IPHONE 15 PRO USER GUIDE

MW00886351

A Complete Step By Step Instruction Manual for Beginners & Seniors to Learn How to Use the New iPhone 15 Pro And Pro Max With iOS Tips & Tricks

BY

HERBERT A. CLARK

Table of Contents

Page |

Page |

Page |

Page |

Page |

Page |

Page |

Page |

Watch memories in the Photos application.....329

Export videos & pictures to an external storage device.....335

FACETIME.....337

Page |

Page |

INTRODUCTION

Released in 2023, the iPhone 15 Pro & iPhone 15 Pro Max are Apple's top-notch phones. The iPhone 15 Pro models have more features than the iPhone 15 & 15 Plus, offering an improved camera, the Action button, the A17 chip, and more.

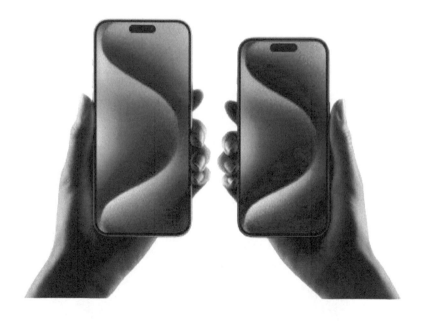

The iPhone 15 Pro models are available in Black, Natural Titanium, Blue, and White colours.

FEATURES OF IPHONE 15 PRO AND PRO MAX

Design

The iPhone 15 Pro models have basically the same design as the iPhone 14 Pro models, but with more streamlined edges that change how the phones feel on your hand.

This year Apple stopped using stainless steel for the Pro models and introduced titanium bands which encompass the glass back & front. Titanium is lighter than stainless steel, so newer models are lighter and the material is more resistant to dents and scratches.

The iPhone 15 Pro measures in at 6.10 inches, while the Pro Max model is 6.70 inches.

The iPhone 15 Pro is 146.60mm tall, 70.60mm wide, 8.250mm thick, & weighs 187g. The iPhone

15 Pro Max is 159.90mm tall, 76.70mm wide, 8.250mm thick & weighs 221g.

The titanium Pro models come in blue, natural titanium, black, and white colour options.

The pill-shaped Dynamic Island continues to sit at the upper part of the iPhone's screen, housing the front-facing camera.

There's a power button on the right side of the phone and an Action button & volume buttons on the left side. The Action button can be set to perform one of different activities; from activating shortcuts to turning on the flashlight, and it can be customized.

Under your device, you'll find a microphone, speaker holes, and a USB-C port.

Dust & water resistance

The iPhone 15 Pro models have an IP68 rating for water & dust resistance. The phones can withstand a depth of 6m (19.70ft) for about thirty minutes.

With an IP68 rating, the iPhone 15 Pro Models can withstand rain, accidental exposure to water, & splashes, but intentional exposure to water should be avoided.

Display

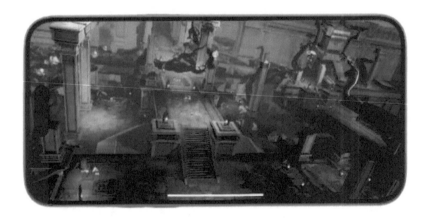

The iPhone 15 Pro models have a Super Retina XDR OLED screen that spans the body of the device. A contrast ratio of 2000000:1 allows for darker blacks & brighter whites, and the iPhone has a maximum brightness of about 2,000 nits outdoors, which makes it easy to see your iPhone's screen in the sun.

The iPhone 15 Pro has a 2556 x 1179 resolution with 460 pixels per inch, while the Pro Max model has a 2796 x 1290 resolution with 460 pixels per inch.

Wide colour compatibility provides clear, life-like colours, & True Tone matches the screen's white balance to the lighting around the phone making the screen more pleasant to look at.

USB-C port

The new iPhone can now be charged with a USB-C cable.

USB-C allows your phone to directly charge an Apple Watch or AirPod with a USB-C cable. Although the charging speed is slow, it is possible to charge another iPhone with the new iPhone 15 Pro and Pro Max.

RAM

The iPhone 15 Pro models have 8 GB RAM.

Storage space

The iPhone 15 Pro's storage space begins at 128GB, while the Pro Max begins at 256 GB. The iPhone 15 Pro and Pro Max are available with as much as 1 TB of storage space

Camera

The iPhone 15 Pro and Pro Max have a 12MP front camera with an f/1.90 aperture that offers better performance for pictures & videos.

There's a 48MP Wide lens on the back of the iPhone 15 Pro and Pro Max, which makes use of 2nd-gen sensor-shift optical picture stabilization. The camera has a focal length of 24 mm and an aperture of f/1.780.

There's also an enhanced 12MP Telephoto camera on the back of the iPhone that offers 5x optical zoom.

Battery Life

The iPhone 15 Pro has a 3274mAh battery, while the Pro Max model is equipped with a 4422mAh battery. The iPhone 15 Pro can last about 23 hours when watching videos, about 20 hours when streaming videos, & about 75 hours when playing music. While the iPhone 15 Pro Max can last about 29 hours when watching videos, about 25 hours when streaming videos, & about 95 hours when playing music.

SETUP YOUR IPHONE

Switch on your phone

Long-press your iPhone's side button till the Apple icon appears on your screen.

Next, you will see "Hello" displayed in different languages. Adhere to the directives on your display to begin your iPhone setup.

Choose the icons & text size on your phone

Move the slider to choose the icons & text size: Large, Medium, or Default. When you are done, click on the **Continue** button

Setup manually or use the Quick-Start feature

You can use the **Quick Start** feature to automatically setup your new phone if you have another device.

If you don't have other devices, touch the **Setup Without Another Device** button.

Activate your phone

Your phone has to be connected to a mobile or WiFi network to activate & proceed with the setup.

Touch one of the WiFi networks to connect to it, or click on the **Continue without WiFi** option to utilize your phone's mobile network.

Setup for yourself or a child

Choose whether to setup the phone for yourself or a child.

Setup Face ID & create a passcode

Adhere to the guidelines on your screen to setup the Face ID feature so that you can use your face to unlock your iPhone & authenticate purchases.

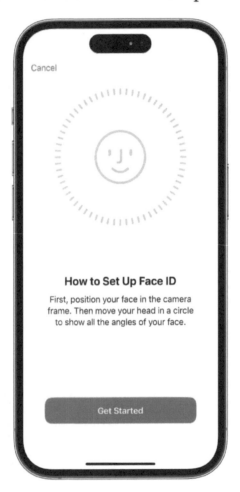

After that, create a 6-digit passcode to protect your information. You need to set a passcode before you can use features like Apple Pay, Face ID, and more. Touch the **Passcode Options** button to see more password options.

Restore or transfer your applications & data

Select how you want to move your data from your old device to your phone.

If there is no available backup or if you do not have other devices, touch the **Don't Transfer Anything** button.

Log in with Apple ID

Insert your Apple ID details in the appropriate fields, or click on the "**Forgot your password or don't have an Apple ID?**" option to create an Apple ID for yourself, configure your Apple ID later, or recover your passcode or Apple ID.

If you have multiple Apple IDs, touch **Other Sign-In Options**, and then click on the **Use Multiple Accounts** option.

After signing in with your Apple ID, your iPhone might request for a verification code from your old device.

Activate automatic updates & setup other features

Adhere to the instructions on your display to allow your iPhone's operating system to update automatically and setup other features, such as mobile service and Apple Pay or a phone number:

❖ You will be asked to setup or activate features & services such as Siri.
❖ After that, adhere to the guidelines on your display to setup Screen-Time, which shows how much time you spend on your phone.

❖ Next, find out which info you can share with Apple & decide whether or not to share info with application developers.
❖ Lastly, touch Dark or Light to show a preview of how your phone adjusts. Choose the **Auto** option to set your device to automatically switch between light & dark throughout the day. Click on the **Continue** button to complete the setup.

BASIC SETTINGS

The iPhone 15 Pro & Pro Max

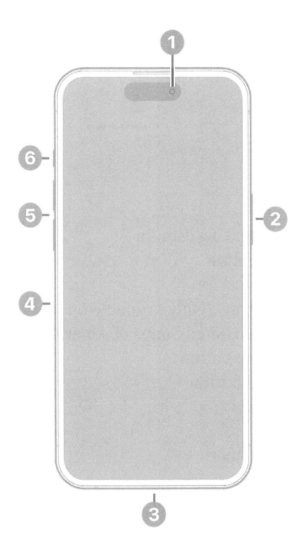

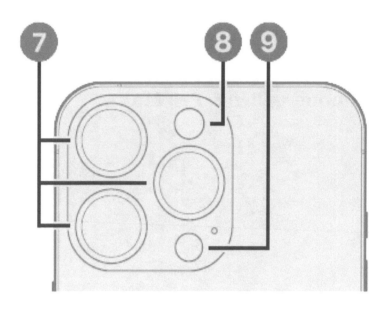

1) The Front-facing camera
2) The Side button
3) USB-C connector
4) SIM card tray. (Only available on models bought outside the United States of America).
5) The Volume button
6) The Action button
7) Back camera
8) Flashlight
9) LiDAR Scanner

Wake your phone

When your iPhone screen turns off, adhere to the guidelines below to wake it:

❖ Press your iPhone's Side button.

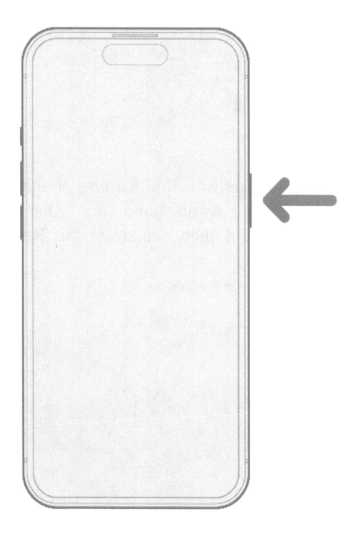

❖ Raise your phone.

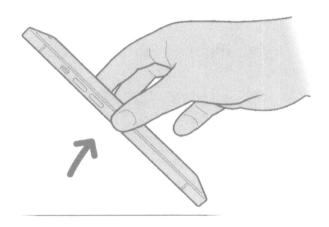

Note: To deactivate this feature, simply enter the Settings application, tap Display & Brightness, and then deactivate the **Raise to Wake** feature.

❖ Tap your iPhone's screen.

Basic gestures

Use the following gestures to interact with your iPhone.

Touch/tap: Gently use a finger to touch what's on your screen. For instance, touch an app's icon on the Apps Library to open the application.

Hold down/long press: Use one of your fingers to press an item on your iPhone's screen till something happens. For instance, long-press the Home Screen's wallpaper to make the apps' icons jiggle.

Swipe: Move one of your fingers across your iPhone's display quickly.

Scroll: Move one of your fingers across your iPhone's display without raising it. For instance, in the Photos application, you can scroll up or down to view your pictures & videos. Swipe to scroll faster; touch your iPhone's display to stop scrolling.

Zoom. Put 2 fingers close to each other on your screen. Spread the fingers apart to zoom in, or drag the fingers close to each other or zoom out.

Or, double-tap a map or picture to zoom in, and tap it twice again to zoom out.

Go to the Home Screen: Swipe up from the lower edge of your iPhone's screen to go back to the Home screen from any application.

App Switcher: Swipe up from the lower edge of your phone display, and pause in the middle of the display to open the Apps Switcher. Swipe to the right to view all the open applications, and touch one of the apps to use it.

Control Center: Swipe-down from the upper right edge of your screen to enter the Controls Center. Long press any of the controls to view options. You can remove or add controls, in the Setting application> Controls Centre.

Move from one open app to another: Swipe right or left along the lower edge of your iPhone's screen to quickly move from one open application to another.

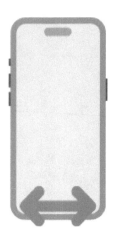

Activate Siri: Say **"Hey Siri"** or **"Siri"**. Or long-press the side button while making a request, then release the button when you are done talking.

Use Accessibility Shortcut. Press the Side button thrice quickly.

Use Emergency SOS. Hold down the side button & one of the volume buttons at the same time till you see the sliders and the Emergency SOS countdown ends, then release both buttons.

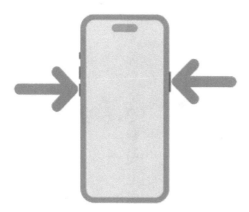

Turn off. Hold down the side button & one of the volume buttons simultaneously till the power off slider appears, and then drag the Power off slider to the right end. Or, enter the Settings application, touch the **General** button, and then click the **Shut Down** button.

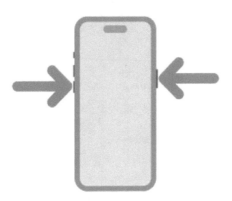

Force restart. Press & release the Increase volume button, press & release the Decrease volume button, and then long-press the Side button till you see the Apple symbol.

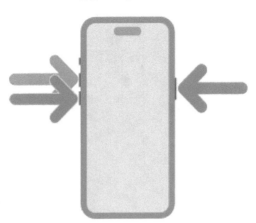

Unlock your iPhone with Face ID

If you activated the **Face ID** feature when setting up your iPhone, adhere to the instructions below to unlock your phone with Face Recognition.

❖ Press the side button, raise your phone, or tap your phone's screen to wake it, and then stare at the screen.
   The lock icon will animate from closed to open to let you know that your device has been unlocked.
❖ Swipe up from the lower edge of your screen.

Press the side button to lock your phone. Your device will automatically lock if the screen is not tapped for about a minute.

Unlock your iPhone with passcode

If you created a password when setting up your phone, adhere to the instructions below to unlock your phone with the passcode you created:

❖ Press the side button, raise your phone, or tap your phone's screen to wake it, and then Swipe up from the lower edge of your iPhone's lock screen.

❖ Insert your passcode

Press the side button to lock your device. Your phone will automatically lock if the screen is not tapped for about a minute.

Find Settings on your phone

You can find the iPhone settings you want to change in the Settings application.

❖ Touch the Settings application's icon  in the Apps Library or your Home Screen.

❖ Swipe down from the upper part of the display to show the search box, and then type a word—"Screen," for instance—then touch one of the settings that appear.

Learn what iPhone status icons mean

The icon in the status bar in the upper part of your display provides info about your phone.

Status icon	Meaning
📶	WIFI: Your device has connected to a WIFI network
..ıll	Cellular signal: if there is no service, you'll see **"No Signal"** in the status bar
::ıll	Dual cellular signals: if you're using two SIMs, you'll see this icon in the upper part of your display. The bars at the top show the signal strength of the SIM you're using for mobile data. While the bars at the bottom indicate the strength of your other SIM.
5G	5G network is available
✈	Airplane mode is active
5G+	A higher frequency version of 5G is available
5G U C	A higher frequency version of 5G is available
5G U W	A higher frequency version of 5G is available
5G E	5G E

E	EDGE
3G	3G network is available
4G	4G network is available
LTE	The LTE network is available
G	1xRTT/GPRS
	Emergency SOS via satellite; your phone is not connected to a WIFI or mobile network, but you can contact the emergency department via satellite.
SOS	SOS only
Wi-Fi	WIFI calling; your phone is setup for WIFI calling
	Personal Hotspot connection: Your phone has connected to the Personal Hotspot of another device
VPN	VPN
	Navigation; Your phone is providing directions to a location
	This icon indicates that your phone is providing Personal Hotspot for another device.
	Phone call
	FaceTime

	Screen recording
	The orange dot indicates that your iPhone's microphone is in use
	The green dot indicates that your iPhone's camera is in use
	Your phone is synchronizing with your computer
	Call forwarding
	Network activity
	DND is enabled
	Your device is locked
	An application is making use of Location Services.
	Your iPhone's display is locked in portrait orientation.
	Headphones connected
	Alarm
	Displays your iPhone's battery level. When the icon's colour changes to yellow, it means Low Power Mode has been activated.
	Battery Charging

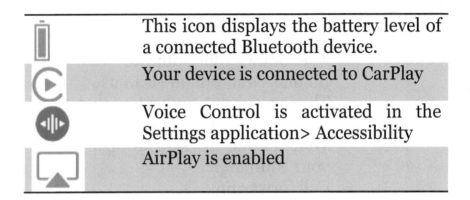

	This icon displays the battery level of a connected Bluetooth device.
	Your device is connected to CarPlay
	Voice Control is activated in the Settings application> Accessibility
	AirPlay is enabled

Setup mobile service on your device

You have to insert a physical SIM or setup an eSIM before your phone can connect to a cellular network. (You can only use an eSIM on iPhone 15 models purchased in the United States) Contact your network carrier to get a SIM & setup mobile service.

Setup an eSIM

Your device can digitally store your carrier-issued eSIM. If your carrier allows **eSIM Quick Transfer** or **eSIM Carrier Activation**, you can switch on your device and adhere to the instructions on your display to activate your eSIM when setting up your phone.

If you've already setup your device, you can carry out any of the below:

- ❖ eSIM Carrier Activation: Some carriers can send a new eSIM directly to the phone; contact your carrier to begin this process. When you're sent the "Finish Cellular Setup" notification, touch it. Or enter the Settings application, touch Cellular, and then touch Add eSIM or Setup Cellular.
- ❖ Quick eSIM transfer: Some network carriers are compatible with moving phone numbers from an old iPhone to a new iPhone without having to contact them.
  On your new iPhone, enter the Settings app, touch Cellular, touch Setup Cellular or Adds eSIM, and then touch the **Transfer From Nearby iPhone** button or pick one of the phone numbers. On your old iPhone, adhere to the directives on your display to confirm the eSIM transfer.
  Note: Your phone number will stop working on your old device after you transfer it to your new iPhone.
- ❖ Scan the QR code: Enter the Settings app, touch the **Cellular** button, touch Add eSIM or Setup

Cellular, and then touch the **Use QR Code** button. (You may have to touch the **Other Options** button first.) Scan the QR code with your device or insert the details manually. You may be told to insert a confirmation code you received from your network carrier.

❖ Porting from another phone: If your previous phone is not an iPhone, contact your network carrier to transfer your number.

❖ Activate service using a network carrier's application: Enter the Apps Store, download the carrier's application, and use the application to activate mobile service.

Install a physical SIM card

Note: iPhone 15 models purchased in the United States do not have a physical SIM port.

❖ Insert a SIM card ejecting tool into the SIM card tray's hole, and then push the toll toward your phone to bring out the SIM tray.

❖ Remove the SIM tray from your device.

❖ Put the SIM card in the tray.

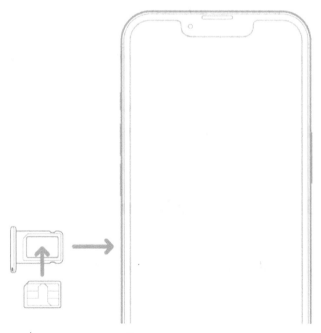

- ❖ Put the tray back in your phone.
- ❖ If you've previously setup a PIN on your SIM, insert the PIN correctly when prompted.
  NOTE: Do not try to guess the SIM PIN. You may lock your SIM completely if you enter the wrong one and you won't be able to make calls or use mobile data until you get a new SIM.

Convert your physical SIM to eSIM

If your network carrier is compatible with it, you can convert a physical SIM to an eSIM.

- ❖ Enter the Settings application, touch Cellular, touch the **Setup Cellular** or the **Add eSIM** button, and select the number with a physical SIM.
- ❖ Click on the **Convert to ESIM** button, and then adhere to the directives on your display.

Use Dual SIM on your iPhone

There are several ways to use Dual SIM:

❖ You can use one of the phone numbers for personal calls and then other number for business
❖ Have separate data plan and voice plan

Setup Dual SIM

❖ Enter the Settings app, touch Cellular, and then ensure you have at least 2 lines in the SIMs section.
❖ Activate two lines— touch one of the lines, and then touch the **Turn On this Line** button.
You can also change settings like SIM PIN, Cellular Plan Label, etc.
❖ Pick a line for mobile data— touch the **Cellular Data** button, and then touch one of the lines. To use either line depending on network availability & coverage, activate the **Allow Mobile Data Switching** feature
❖ Choose a line for calls —touch the **Default Voice Line** button, and then touch one of the lines.

Connect your iPhone to the Internet

You can use a WIFI or mobile network to connect your phone to the internet.

Connect your phone to WiFi

❖ Enter the Settings application, touch the **WIFI** button, and then activate WIFI.
❖ Touch any of the below:
  ➢ A network: Type the passcode, if needed.
  ➢ Other: To join a hidden network, simply type the network's name, security type & passcode.

If the WiFi icon appears in the upper part of your display, it means your iPhone has connected to WiFi. (To confirm this, enter the **Safari** application, and visit a website).

Join a Personal Hotspot

If an iPhone or iPad is sharing Personal Hotspot, you can use its mobile internet connection.

❖ Enter the Settings app, touch WiFi, and then touch the name of the device that's sharing its Hotspot.
❖ If your iPhone asks you to enter a password, type the password displayed in the Settings

application> Cellular> Personal Hotspot on the device that's sharing the Hotspot.

Connect your iPhone to a mobile network

If WiFi is not available, your phone will automatically connect to your carrier's mobile data network. If your iPhone does not connect, check the below:

- ❖ Make sure your SIM is active & unlocked.
- ❖ Enter the Settings application> Cellular
- ❖ Make sure Cellular Data is activated. If you are using two SIM cards, click on the **Cellular Data** button, then check the line selected.

Manage Apple ID settings

The account you use to gain access to Apple services (like iMessage, iCloud, Face-Time, Apps Store, etc.) is known as your Apple ID.

Sign in with your Apple ID

If you did not sign in when setting up your iPhone, simply adhere to the directives below:

- ❖ Enter the Settings application.
- ❖ Touch the **Sign in to your iPhone** button
- ❖ Type your Apple ID details in the appropriate boxes
  If you do not have an Apple ID, you can set up one for yourself
- ❖ If your account is protected with 2-factor authentication, type the 6-digit verification code.

Change your Apple ID settings

- ❖ Enter the Settings application, and touch [your name].
- ❖ Carry out any of the below:
  - ➢ Update your profile
  - ➢ Change your passcode
  - ➢ Update your payment methods
  - ➢ Use iCloud
  - ➢ View & manage your subscriptions
  - ➢ Manage Family Sharing
  - ➢ Remove or add Account Recovery Contacts

Use iCloud on iPhone

ICloud securely stores your files, backups, videos, pictures, etc. automatically. iCloud gives you 5GB of free storage space & an e-mail account.

Change iCloud settings

Log in with your Apple ID, and then carry out any of the below:

❖ Enter the Settings application, touch [your name], and then touch iCloud.

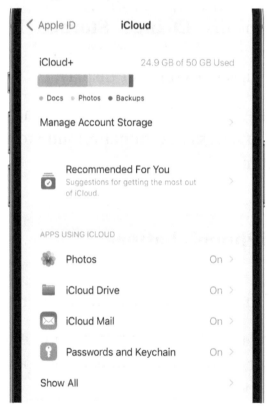

❖ Carry out any of the below:
  ➢ Check your iCloud storage space.
  ➢ Activate the features you'd like to use, like iCloud Backup, iCloud Drive, & Photos.

Update, change or cancel your iCloud+ subscription

❖ Enter the Settings application, touch [your name], and then touch iCloud.
❖ Click on the **Manage Storage Account button**, touch the **Change Storage Plan** button, select one of the options, and then adhere to the directives on your display.

Note: If you cancel your iCloud+ subscription, you will not be able to access additional iCloud storage and iCloud+ features.

Charge your iPhone's battery

Carry out any of the below to charge your iPhone:

❖ Use a charging cable to connect your phone to a power adapter and then connect the power adapter to the power outlet.

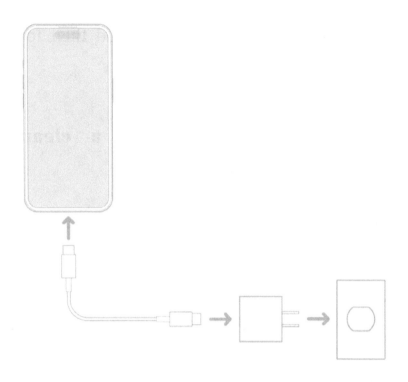

Optimize iPhone battery charging

Your phone has settings that help to slow your battery's aging rate by reducing the time it takes to fully charge. This feature makes use of machine learning to understand your daily charging patterns and then waits until it's close to when you need your phone before it charges past 80 percent.

❖ Enter the Settings application, touch Battery, and then touch Battery Health and Charging.

❖ Touch Charging Optimization, and then touch Optimized Battery Charging.

Charge your iPhone with a cleaner energy source (US only)

With the **Clean Energy Charging** feature, your phone makes use of a forecast of the carbon emissions from the local power grid to charge when cleaner energy is available. Your device learns from your daily charging schedule so it can fully charge before you use it.

❖ Enter the Settings application, and then touch Battery.
❖ Click on Battery Health & Charging, and then activate the Clean Energy Charging feature

Show your iPhone's battery percentage in the status bar

You can see how much is left in your iPhone's battery in the status bar.

Adhere to the directives below to activate this feature:

Enter the Settings application, touch Battery, and then activate the **Battery Percentage** feature.

Review your phone battery health

Enter the Settings application, touch Battery, and then touch Battery Health & Charging.

You will see info about your iPhone's battery capacity, peak performance, and more.

See battery usage information

Enter the Settings application, and then touch Battery.

Use low power mode to reduce your iPhone's power consumption

Low Power Mode will reduce how much power your iPhone uses when the battery is low.

Note: iPhone may perform some tasks more slowly in low power mode.

Low Power Mode activates automatically when your iPhone's battery is low and automatically deactivates when the battery charges to a certain level.

Use one of the methods below to activate or deactivate Low Power Mode:

❖ In the Settings application: Enter the Settings application, and then touch Battery.

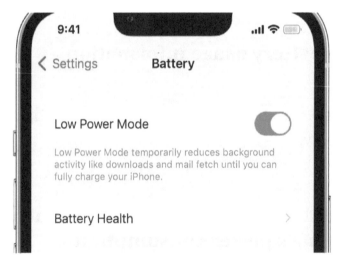

❖ In the Control Centre: Swipe down from the upper right corner of your display to open the

Controls Centre, and then click the Low Power Mode button .

(If you can't find the Low Power Mode button , add it to the Controls Centre—enter the Settings application, touch Controls Centre, and then click the Add icon beside Low Power Mode.)

Adjust your iPhone's volume

Press the buttons on the side of your phone to change the volume level.

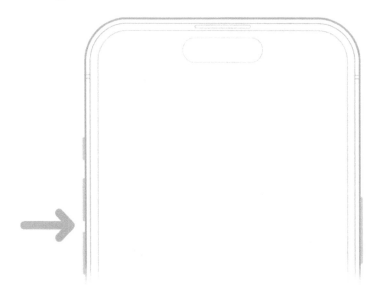

Adjust your iPhone's volume in the Controls Centre

You can change your iPhone's volume level in the Controls Centre.

Swipe down from the upper right corner of your phone's display to open the Controls Centre, and drag the volume slider 🔊.

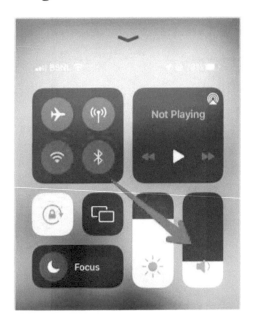

Reduce loud headphone sounds

- ❖ Enter the Settings application, click on Sound and Haptics, and then touch Headphone Safety.
- ❖ Activate Reduce Loud Sound, and then slide the slider to set the maximum volume.

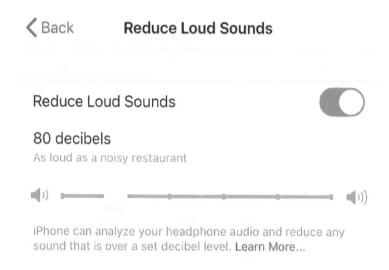

Temporarily silence calls & alerts

Swipe down from the upper right corner of your phone's display to open the Controls Centre, touch the **Focus** button, and then touch the **Do Not Disturb** option.

Launch applications on your phone

You can quickly launch apps from the home screen or the app library.

❖ To go to your iPhone's Home screen, simply swipe up from the lower edge of your display.

❖ Swipe to the left to view applications on the other Home Screen pages.

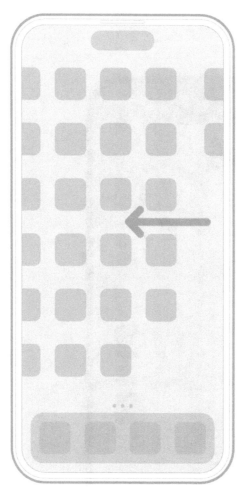

❖ Swipe left continuously until you pass all the Home Screen pages to enter the Apps Library, where your applications are arranged by category.

❖ Touch an app's icon to launch the application.

❖ Swipe up from the lower edge of your screen to go back to the Apps Library.

Apps Library

The Apps Library displays your applications organized into categories like Information & Reading, Utilities, etc. The applications you use very often can be found at the top of the Apps

Library and at the top of the category they are in, so you can easily find & launch them.

Note: The applications in the Apps Library are categorized according to how you use your applications. You can add applications from the Apps Library to the Home Screen but you cannot change an app's category in the Apps Library.

Find & launch an application in the Apps Library

❖ Swipe up from the lower edge of your display to go to your iPhone's Home Screen, and then swipe left continuously until you pass all your Home Screen pages to enter the Apps Library.
❖ Touch the search box in the upper part of the Apps Library, and then type the name of the application you are looking for. Or simply scroll to look for the application.
❖ Touch an app's icon to launch the application.

Hide & show Home Screen pages

Since you can find all your applications in the Apps Library, there might not be any need for many

Home Screen pages. You can decide to hide some of the Home Screen pages, which will bring the Apps Library closer to the 1st Home Screen page.

- ❖ Long-press one of the Home Screen pages till the applications start jiggling.
- ❖ Touch the dots in the lower part of your display. Next, you will see thumbnail pictures of your iPhone Home Screen pages with checkmarks under them.

❖ To hide a Home Screen page, simply touch to remove the checkmark under the page.
To show a page you've hidden, touch to add the checkmark.

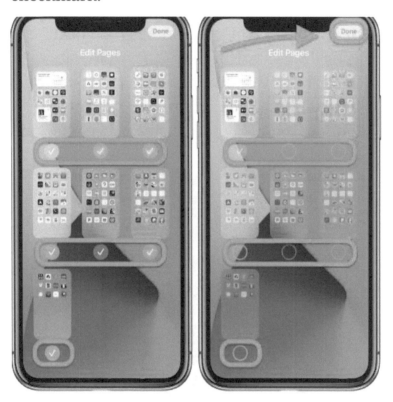

❖ Touch the **Done** button when you're done.

Rearrange Home Screen pages

You can change the order of your Home Screen pages. For example, you can put your favourite applications on one Home Screen page, and then make it your first page.

❖ Long-press one of the Home Screen pages till the applications start jiggling.
❖ Touch the dots in the lower part of your display. Next, you will see thumbnail pictures of your iPhone Home Screen pages with checkmarks under them.

❖ To move a page, long-press the page, and then drag the Home Screen page to another location on your screen.

❖ Touch the **Done** button two times.

Change the download location for new apps

When you download applications from the Apps Store, you can add the applications to the Apps Library & Home Screen, or only the Apps Library.

❖ Enter the Settings application, and then touch Home Screen & Apps Library.
❖ Choose one of the options in the **Newly Downloaded Apps** section

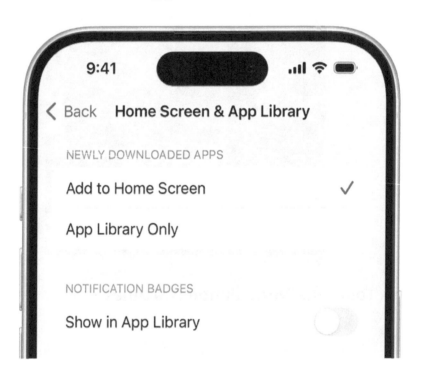

App Switcher

Open the Apps Switcher to easily switch between open applications on your phone.

Adhere to the directives below to open the Apps Switcher:

- ❖ Swipe up from the lower edge of your display, and then stop in the middle of your display.
- ❖ Swipe right to view all your open applications, and then touch the application you'd like to use.

Switch between open applications

Swipe left or right along the lower edge of your display to quickly move from one open application to another.

Move an application from the Apps Library to the Home Screen

Long press the app's icon in the Apps Library, and then touch the **Add to Home Screen** button.

The application will appear in the Apps Library and on the Home Screen.

Quit an application

To quit an app, swipe up from the lower edge of your display, and then pause in the middle of your display to open the Apps Switcher, swipe right to find the application, and swipe up on the application.

Multitask with Picture in Picture

With the **Picture in Picture** feature, you can watch videos or make a FaceTime call while using other applications.

While watching a video, click on the Video Zoom button .

The video window will shrink to one of the corners of your screen to create space for the Home Screen so that you can launch other applications. With the video window showing, you can:

❖ Change the size of the video window: To increase the size of the video window, simply pinch open on the window. Pinch closed to shrink the window again.

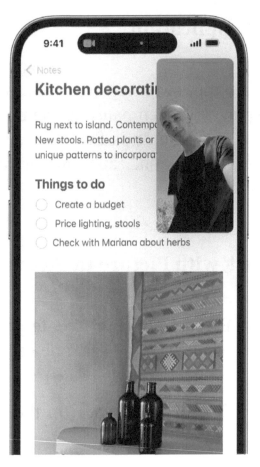

❖ Hide & display controls: Touch the video window.

❖ Move the window: Simply drag the window to any corner of your display.

❖ Hide the video window: Drag the window off the right or left edge of your display.

❖ Touch the Close icon ⊗ to close the video window.

❖ Touch the Full-screen icon  in the window to return the window to full screen.

Access features from your iPhone's Lock Screen

The Lock screen is the first screen you see when you wake your phone. Even when your phone is locked, you can quickly gain access to useful features & info from your iPhone's Lock Screen. Carry out any of the below from the lock screen:

❖ Media playback control: Use the playback controls on your iPhone's lock screen to fast-forward, rewind, pause, or play media playing on your phone

❖ Swipe left on the Lock Screen to use your iPhone's Camera. You can also long-press the Camera button 📷, and then release your finger.
❖ Swipe down from the upper right corner of your display to open the Controls Centre
❖ Swipe up from the middle of your display to show earlier notifications
❖ Swipe right to see more widgets

Display notification previews on your iPhone's Lock Screen

❖ Enter the Settings application, and touch Notifications.
❖ Touch the **Show Previews** button and then touch the **Always** button.
❖ Select how you want notifications to be displayed on your phone lock screen:
  ➢ Choose the **List** option to make your phone display the notifications in a list.
  ➢ Touch the **Stack** option to show the notifications grouped into stacks by application
  ➢ Choose the **Count** option to show only the number of notifications.

Perform quick actions from the home screen & Apps Library

You can long-press an app in the Apps Library or Home Screen to open the quick actions menu.

For instance:

❖ Long-press the Notes application icon , and then touch the **New Checklist** button in the menu that appears

❖ Touch & hold the Maps application icon , and then touch the **Mark My Location** button in the menu that appears

❖ Touch & hold the Camera application icon and then touch the **Video** button in the menu that appears.

Note: If you long-press an application for too long before selecting one of the quick actions, all the apps will start jiggling. Click on the **Done** button, and then try again.

View Previews and other quick menus

❖ In the Photos application, long-press a picture to preview it and display a list of options.
❖ In the Mail application, long-press an email in one of the mailboxes to preview the content of the message and view a list of options.

- ❖ Open the Controls Centre, then long-press an item like the Camera app icon to see options.
- ❖ On your iPhone's Lock Screen, long-press one of the notifications to respond to it.
- ❖ While typing, use a finger to long-press the Space bar to change the on-screen keyboard to a trackpad.

Search with Spotlight

You can search for applications, contacts, and contents in some applications on your phone. You can also find & open websites, applications, and pictures in your photos library & on the internet.

Select which applications to include in Search

- ❖ Head over to the Settings application, and touch Siri & Search.
- ❖ Scroll down, tap any of the applications, and then activate or disable **Show App in Search**.

Search on iPhone

❖ Swipe down on the Lock Screen or Home Screen or click on the Search button `Q Search` in the lower part of your iPhone's Home Screen.

❖ Type what you want in the search box.
❖ Carry out any of the below:
  ➢ Click on the Go or Search button to start your search.
  ➢ Click on one of the suggested sites to visit it
  ➢ Touch one of the suggested applications to open it.
  ➢ Learn more about a search suggestion: Touch it, and then touch a result to open it.
  ➢ Click on the Clear Text button ⊗ to clear the search box

Search in applications

A lot of applications have a search box or a search icon so that you can easily find something in the application.

- In an application, touch the Search icon Q or the search field
  If you can't find the Search icon or search field, simply swipe down front the top of the app.
- Type what you want in the search box, and then touch the **Search** button

See the total storage and storage used for each application on your device

Enter the Settings application, touch General, and then touch iPhone Storage.

Learn more about your iPhone

Enter the Settings application, touch General, and then touch the **About** button

Activate Airplane mode

Swipe down from the upper right corner of your iPhone display to reveal the Controls Centre, and then click on the **Airplane Mode** button ✈.

Tap to turn on
airplane mode.

You'll see the **Airplane Mode** icon ✈ in the status bar when Airplane Mode is enabled.

Activate or deactivate WiFi or Bluetooth

❖ Swipe-down from the upper right corner of your iPhone's display to show the Controls Center

❖ Click on the WiFi button 📶 to activate WiFi or click on the Bluetooth button ✳ to activate Bluetooth

Tap to turn on Bluetooth.

Tap to turn on Wi-Fi.

Click on the WiFi button 📶 once more to deactivate WiFi or touch the Bluetooth button 🔵 again to deactivate Bluetooth in the Controls Center.

Tap to turn off Bluetooth in airplane mode.

Tap to turn off Wi-Fi in airplane mode.

Call an emergency number when your device is locked

❖ Tap on the **Emergency** button on the Passcode screen

❖ Dial the emergency number(for instance, 911 in the United States), and then click on the Call button 📞

Calculator

You can perform arithmetic, trigonometric, logarithmic, & exponential calculations in the Calculator app.

To use the scientific calculator, just turn your device to landscape orientation.

Copy, clear, or delete numbers

* Copy calculation results: Long-press the calculation result on your screen, touch the **Copy** button, and then paste the result into another application.
* To delete the last number, simply swipe right or left on your screen at the top.
* Clear the screen: Touch the Clear(C) button to clear the last entry or click the All Clear (**AC**) button to erase all entries.

See the time in other cities around the world

You can check the time in different places around the world.

❖ Enter the Clock application, and then touch the **Work Clock** tab in the lower part of your display.
❖ Do any of the below to manage your cities list:

- ➢ Add a city: Touch the Add icon ✛ in the upper part of your display and then select one of the cities.
- ➢ To delete one of the cities, click on the **Edit** button, and then click on the Remove icon ⊖
- ➢ Rearrange the cities: Touch the **Edit** button, and then drag the Rearrange icon ☰ down or up.
- ❖ When you are done, click on the **Done** button.

Set an alarm

- ❖ Enter the Clock application, touch the **Alarms** tab in the lower part of your display, and then touch the Add icon ✛ in the upper part of your display.
- ❖ Set the time, and then select any of the options below:
  - ➢ Repeat: Pick the days you want the alarm to be active.
  - ➢ Snooze: Give yourself some time to rest
  - ➢ Sound: Select a ringing tone, song, or vibration
  - ➢ Label

❖ Click on the **Save** button

Touch the alarm time to edit the alarm. Or click on the **Edit** button in the upper left part of your display and then touch the alarm time.

Touch the button beside the alarm time to turn off the alarm

To delete an alarm, swipe the alarm to the left, and then click on the **Delete** button

Measure someone's height with your phone

You can use the Measure application to measure someone's height.

❖ Set your device in a way that the individual you want to measure can be seen clearly on your display from head to toe.
After a while, a line will appear on top of the individual's head, and the person's height measurement will be displayed under the line.

❖ Touch the Capture button ○ to snap a picture of the measurement.

❖ To save the image, click on the screenshot's thumbnail in the bottom left part of the screen, click on the **Done** button, and then select one of the options to save it on your phone.

Use your phone as a level

You can use your device to check whether nearby objects are flat, straight, or level.

❖ Launch the Measure app.

❖ Click on the **Level** tab in the lower part of your display, and then hold your phone against an object, like a frame.

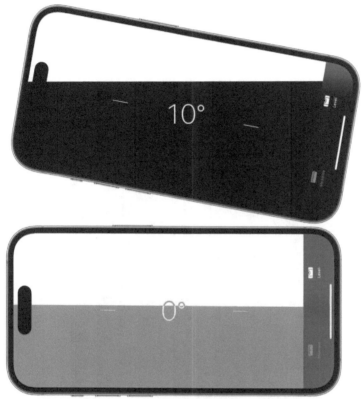

➤ Make an item level: Rotate your device & the object till your iPhone's display shows green.
➤ Match the slope: Touch your screen to snap the slope of the first object. Hold your device firmly against the other object & rotate your phone & the object till your display shows green.

Touch your display to reset the level.

Use the compass on your phone

The compass application shows you the direction your device is pointing to, your location, and your altitude.

The bearings, coordinates, and altitude of your phone are displayed in the lower part of your screen.

Touch the coordinates in the lower part of your display to show your location in the Maps app.

PERSONALIZE THE ACTION BUTTON

Your new device has an Action button instead of a Silent/Ring switch. You can select the function you want the button to perform when it's pressed.

Personalize the Action button

❖ Head over to the Settings application, and then click on Action Button.
You'll see a picture of the iPhone's side with icons that represent actions you can perform with the Action button.

❖ To pick one of the actions, simply swipe to the one you want—its name will appear under the dot.

❖ If there're more options for the action you chose, a Menu button ⌄ will appear under the action; touch it to view a list of options.

For the Accessibility & Shortcut actions, you must touch the blue button under the action and choose one of the options—if not, the Action button won't perform any action.

Use the Action button

Long-press the Action button to perform the action assigned to it.

For a lot of functions, the Action button can be used to activate or deactivate a setting. For instance, if the action you chose is Silent Mode, you can long-press the Action button to activate Silent Mode 🔕. If you long-press the Action button again, it will deactivate Silent Mode.

DYNAMIC ISLAND

A Voice Memo
recording in progress

You can check notifications & current activities — like music playing, Voice Memos recording in progress, & Maps directions— in the Dynamic Island. The Dynamic Island can be found in the upper part of your screen whenever your phone is unlocked.

You can carry out any of the below in the Dynamic Island:

* Enlarge the activity to view more details: Long-press the activity or swipe from the middle to the left or right side
* Move from one activity to another: Swipe from one side or the other
* Make the Dynamic Island smaller again: Swipe from the left or right side toward the middle.

PERSONALIZE YOUR DEVICE

Change your iPhone vibrations & sounds

Change the sound your device plays when you receive an email, call, reminder, voicemail, or any other type of notification.

Set vibration & sound options

❖ Head over to the Settings application and click on Sound & Haptics.

❖ Drag the slider in the Ringtone & Alert Volume section to set the volume for all sounds on your phone.

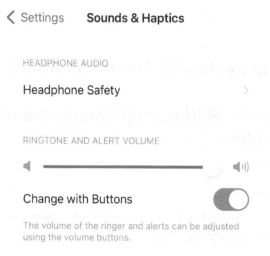

⟨ Settings   **Sounds & Haptics**

HEADPHONE AUDIO

Headphone Safety   ⟩

RINGTONE AND ALERT VOLUME

🔇 ——————————————— 🔊

Change with Buttons   ⬤

The volume of the ringer and alerts can be adjusted using the volume buttons.

❖ To set the vibration & tones pattern for sounds, click on one of the sound types, like text tone or ringtone.
❖ Carry out any of the below:
  ➢ Pick one of the tones (scroll to check out all of them).
    Ringtones are for calls, clock timers, & alarm; text tones are for messages, voicemail, & other notifications
  ➢ Touch the **Vibration** button, then choose one of the vibration patterns, or touch the **Create New Vibration** button to create one for yourself.

You can also change the sound your device plays for certain individuals. Enter the Contacts application, touch the name of an individual, touch the **Edit** button, and then pick a text tone and ringing tone.

Activate or disable haptic feedback

❖ Enter the Settings application, and touch Sound & Haptics.
❖ Activate or disable Systems Haptics
  When you disable System Haptics, you will not feel or hear vibrations from incoming notifications & calls.

Change your phone's wallpaper

❖ Head over to the Settings application, click on the **Wallpaper** button, and then tap the **Add New Wallpaper** button.

Next, you will see the wallpaper gallery

❖ Carry out any of the below:
  ➢ Click on one of the buttons in the upper part of the wallpaper gallery—like Live Photos, Emoji, etc.—to decorate your wallpaper with one of your pictures, an emoji pattern, etc.

  ➢ Pick one of the wallpapers from any of the featured collections (Weather, Astronomy, etc.).
❖ Touch the **Add** button, and then do any of the below:
  ➢ Touch the **Set as Wallpaper Pair** button to use the wallpaper on your Lock & Home Screen.
  ➢ Make more adjustments to the Home Screen: Touch the **Customize Home Screen** button. Touch one of the colors to change the colour of the wallpaper, touch the Photos icon

🖼 to use one of your pictures, or touch the **Blur** button to blur the wallpaper so that the applications can stand out.

Have your device play a sound effect when it is switched off & on

❖ Enter the Settings app, click on Accessibility, and then click on Audio/Visual.
❖ Activate or disable Power On and Off Sound.

Change the screen brightness manually

Adhere to the instructions below to change your iPhone's screen brightness manually:

❖ Swipe-down from the upper right corner of your screen to reveal the Controls Center, and then drag the Brightness slide ☀ down or up.
❖ Enter the Settings app, click on Display & Brightness, and then drag the slider.

Activate or disable Dark Mode

The Dark mode feature gives your phone display a dark colour scheme that is ideal for low-light environments.

Do one of the below:

❖ Swipe down from the upper right corner of your iPhone display to reveal the Controls Centre, press & hold the Brightness slide ☀, and then click on the Dark Mode icon ◐ to enable or deactivate Dark Mode.

❖ Enter the Settings app, click on Display & Brightness, and then click on Dark to activate the Dark Mode, or click on Light to disable it.

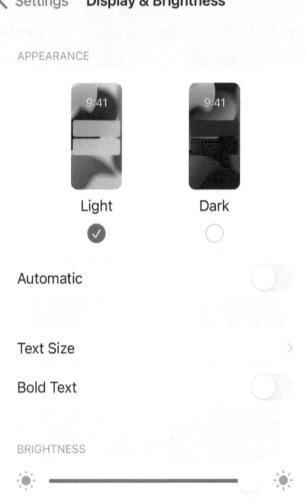

Adjust the screen brightness automatically

Your device uses an inbuilt ambient light sensor to adjust the screen's brightness to match current lighting conditions.

❖ Head over to the Settings app, and then touch Accessibility.
❖ Click on Display and Text Size, and then enable **Auto-Brightness**.

Set Dark Mode to activate or deactivate automatically

You can programme the Dark Mode to automatically activate at specific times (in the night or on a custom schedule).

❖ Head over to the Settings app, and then touch Display & Brightness.
❖ Activate Automatic, and then click on Options.
❖ Click on **Custom Schedule** or **Sunset to Sunrise**.

If you selected the **Custom Schedule** option, click on the options to select when you want Dark Mode to activate & turn off.

If you pick the **Sunset to Sunrise** option, your phone will use the information from your clock & location to determine when it is night for you.

Activate or disable Night Shift

The Night Shift feature can be useful when you are in a dark room in daytime.

Swipe down from the upper right corner of your screen to enter the Controls Centre, long-press the Brightness button ☀, and then click on the Night Shift button ☀ .

Set Night Shift to activate or deactivate automatically

Set Night Shift to change the colours on your screen to the warmer side of the spectrum at night and make looking at the screen more pleasant to the eyes.

- ❖ Head over to the Settings app, click on Display & Brightness, and then click on the **Night Shift** button.
- ❖ Activate **Scheduled**
- ❖ To change the colour balance for Night Shift, slide the slider under Colour Temperature to the cooler or warmer side of the spectrum.

- ❖ Touch the **From** button, and then click on **Custom Schedule** or **Sunset to Sunrise**.

  If you pick the Custom Schedule option, touch the options to select when you want Night Shift to activate & turn off.

  If you choose the **Sunset to Sunrise** option, your phone will use the information from your clock & location to determine when it is night for you.

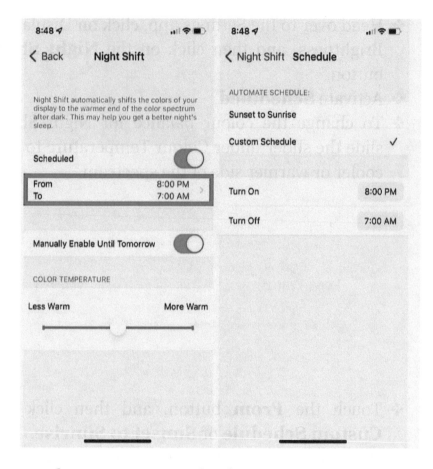

Note: The Sunset to Sunrise feature is not available if you deactivate Location Service in the Settings app> Privacy and Security, or if you deactivate Settings Time Zone in the Settings application> Privacy and Security> Location Service> Systems Service.

Activate or disable True Tone

The **True Tone** feature automatically adjusts your phone display's colour & intensity to match the lighting around you.

Do any of the below:

❖ Swipe down from the upper right corner of your phone display to reveal the Controls Centre, long-press the Brightness button ☀, and then click on the True Tone button ☀.
❖ Enter the Settings app, tap Display and Brightness, and then activate or disable True Tone.

Make your iPhone display On longer

Your device screen will remain On while you are staring at it, but it will dim & eventually lock when you look away for some time. If you want the screen to stay On longer, you can change the duration.

Enter the Settings app, touch the **Display and Brightness** button, touch the **AutoLock** button, and then select the duration.

Always On Display

The Always On feature allows a darkened version of your Lock Screen to remain visible, even when your phone is locked so that you can look at your screen any time to see important info, like the time, date, etc.

This feature is activated by default. To disable it, enter the Settings application, touch Display and Brightness, and then deactivate the **Always On Display** feature.

Use StandBy to check info at a distance while your device is charging

Use the StandBy feature to turn your phone into a bedside clock, a digital picture frame, etc.

Start Standby

❖ Enter the Settings application, touch StandBy, and ensure StandBy is activated.
❖ Connect your phone to its charger and place it on its side; make sure it's stationary and charging.
❖ Press the side button
❖ Swipe right or left to switch between clocks, pictures, & widgets. Swipe down or up to change the options for these views.

When Night Mode is enabled for StandBy, your iPhone's display adapts to the dim light of the night and appears in a red tint so that it does not disturb you while you sleep.

Deactivate StandBy

Head over to the Settings app, touch StandBy, and then disable the **StandBy** feature.

Change your iPhone's name

You can change your iPhone's name, which is used by your Hotspot, AirDrop, your PC, & iCloud.

* ❖ Enter the Settings application, click General, touch About, and then touch Name.
* ❖ Touch the Clear Text button⊗, type a name, and then touch the **Done** button.

Increase the size of items on your screen

* ❖ Enter the Settings app, click on Display & Brightness, and then tap Display Zoom.
* ❖ Click on Lager Text to increase the size of the items on your display.
* ❖ Touch the **Done** button in the top right corner of your screen, and then click on the **Use Zoomed** button.

Change the region & language on your phone

- ❖ Enter the Settings app, tap General, and then tap Language & Region.
- ❖ Set the following:
  - ➢ Your iPhone's language
  - ➢ How you like to be addressed. (Select neutral, masculine, or feminine)
  - ➢ Calendar Format
  - ➢ Temperature unit
  - ➢ Measurement system
  - ➢ The Region
  - ➢ First day of the week
  - ➢ Live text

Organize your applications in folders

Arrange applications into folders to make it easy to look for them on your Home Screen.

Create folders

- ❖ Long-press the background of your iPhone's Home Screen until the applications start vibrating.

❖ Drag one application unto another application to create a folder.

❖ Drag more applications into the folder.
The folder can have more than one page

❖ To change the name of the folder, long-press the folder, touch the **Rename** button, and then type a name.
If the applications start vibrating, tap the background of your iPhone's Home Screen and try again.

❖ When you are done, tap the **Done** button, and then touch the Home Screen two times.

To delete a folder from your iPhone, open the folder, and then drag all the applications out of the folder. The folder will be erased automatically.

Move an application from a folder to the Home Screen

❖ Open the folder on your Home Screen
❖ Long-press the application in the folder till all the applications start jiggling
❖ Drag the application from the folder to your Home Screen.

Add, edit, & remove widgets

Widgets are a way to see current info—today's headlines, your iPhone's battery level, weather report, etc. You can browse widgets in Today's View and add them to your Lock Screen or Home Screen to make this info easily accessible.

You can interact with a widget on your phone without launching its application—for instance; you can touch the Play icon on the Music widget to play a song without opening the Music application.

Add a widget to your Home Screen

❖ Enter the Home Screen page where you'd like to add a widget, then long-press the wallpaper of the Home Screen till all the applications start jiggling.

❖ Touch the Add Widget icon ➕ in the upper part of your display to show the widget gallery.

❖ Scroll to find the widget you're looking for, or search for it, touch it, and then swipe right or left to choose one of the sizes.

- ❖ When you find the size you like, touch the **Add Widget** button.
- ❖ While the applications are still vibrating, drag the widget anywhere on the Home Screen, and then touch the **Done** button.

Interact with widgets

Simply touch a Widget on your Home Screen or Lock Screen to perform a task—for instance; touch the Play icon in the Podcast widget to listen to an episode—without having to open the application.

Edit a widget

- ❖ Long-press a widget on your Home Screen to see the quick actions menu.
- ❖ Click on the **Edit [widget name]** button or the **Edit Stack** button if it is a Smart Stack, and then select from the available options.
- ❖ Touch the **Done** button

Remove a widget from your Home Screen

- ❖ Long-press a widget on your Home Screen to see the quick actions menu.

❖ Click on the **Remove Widget** button (or the **Remove Stack** button), and then click on the **Remove** button.

Check out widgets in Today View

To see widgets in Today's View, simply swipe right from the left edge of your iPhone's Home Screen, and then scroll down & up.

Check out widgets in Today's View & Search when your device is locked

* Enter the Settings app, touch Face ID & Passcode, and type your passcode.
* Activate Today's View & Search in the Allow Access When Locked section

Move applications & widgets around your phone Home Screen

You can change your Home Screen's layout by moving widgets & applications around, dragging them to other Home Screen pages, etc.

* Long-press a widget or an application's icon on your Home Screen, and then click on the **Edit Home Screen** option.
  The applications will start jiggling.
* Drag an application to any of the locations below:
  * Another Home Screen page

You can move a widget or application to another page by dragging it to the right edge of the current Home Screen page. You might have to wait for a few seconds for the next page to appear. The dots close to the Dock indicate how many pages you have & which one you are currently in.

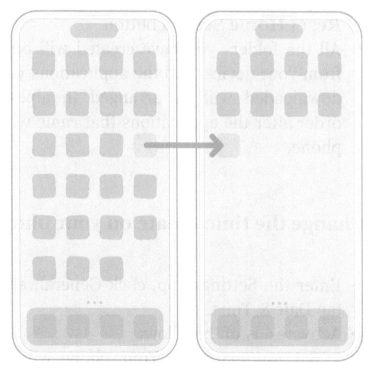

> A different location in the same Home Screen page
❖ When you are done, simply touch the **Done** button.

Reset the Home Screen & applications to their original settings

❖ Head over to the Settings application, tap General, and then tap Transfer or Reset iPhone.
❖ Touch the **Reset** button, click the **Reset Home Screen Layout** button, and then touch the **Reset Home Screen** button
All the folders you have created will be erased from your device, and the applications you have downloaded will be arranged in alphabetical order after the applications that came with your phone.

Change the time & date on your phone

❖ Enter the Settings app, click General, and then tap Date & Time.
❖ Activate any of the below:
  ➢ Set Automatically: Your phone will get the accurate time over the network & your time zone.
  ➢ 24-Hour: Your phone will show the hours from 0-23

To change the default time & date displayed on your phone, disable the **Set Automatically** option, then make the changes

Uninstall applications from your phone

Carry out any of the below:

❖ Delete an application from your Home Screen: Long-press the application on your Home Screen, touch the **Remove Apps** option, and then touch the **Remove from Home Screen** button to leave the application in the Apps Library, or touch the **Delete Apps** option to remove the application from your phone.
❖ Remove an application from the Apps Library & Home Screen: Long-press the application in the Application Library, touch the **Delete Application** button, and then touch the **Delete** button.

If you change your mind, you can download the applications you have deleted from your phone again.

Use & personalize the Control Center

The Controls Centre gives you fast & easy access to useful controls like Media Control, DND, the Cellular Data switch, and some applications.

To open the Controls Centre, simply swipe-down from the upper right edge of the screen. Swipe up from the lower edge of your iPhone's display to exit the Controls Centre.

Access more controls in the Control Center

A lot of controls have additional options. Long press one of the controls to view the available options. For instance, you can:

❖ Long-press the upper left set of controls, and then touch the AirDrop icon to display the AirDrop options.
❖ Long-press the Flashlight button to choose the torch's brightness level
❖ Long-press the Camera button to snap a picture, or record a video.

Touch and hold to
see Camera options.

Add & configure controls

Personalize the Controls Centre by adding shortcuts
to applications and more controls.

❖ Launch the Settings app and then touch the
Controls Centre button.

❖ Click on the Remove button ⊖ or the Add button ⊕ beside a control to remove or add the control

❖ To reorganize the controls, touch the Edit icon ≡ beside a control and then drag it to another location.

Disable access to the Controls Centre in applications

Enter the Settings application, click on the **Controls Centre** button, and then deactivate Access Within Apps.

Change or lock the screen orientation

A lot of applications look different when your device is rotated.

You can lock your iPhone's screen orientation so that it does not change when your phone is rotated.

Swipe down from the upper right corner of your display to open the Controls Center, and then touch the Screen Orientation button 🔒.

When you enable screen orientation, the Orientation Lock icon 🔒 will appear in the status bar.

Focus

The Focus feature can be very helpful when you want to concentrate on certain tasks and set boundaries. You can personalize a provided Focus option—like Sleep, or Personal— or create a Focus mode for yourself. You can use a Focus mode to silence all notifications, or allow only notifications relevant to your situation and let other individuals & applications know you are busy.

When you link a Focus mode to one of your Lock Screens, you can activate the Focus by just swiping to the Lock Screen.

Setup a Focus

❖ Enter the Settings application, click on Focus, and then touch one of the Focus options, such as Work, Sleep, Personal, etc.

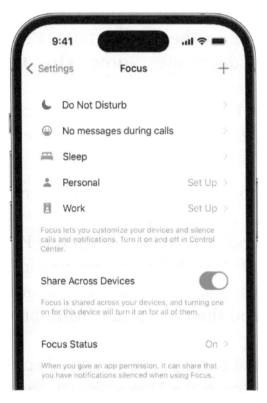

You can set the options described in the steps below for your chosen focus, but you do not have to setup all of them.

❖ Choose the individuals and applications that can send you notifications when the Focus mode is enabled.

After specifying the individuals and applications to allow notifications from, you'll see an Options link.

❖ Click on **Options**, and then carry out any of the below:

   ➢ Show silent notifications on your Lock Screen or send them to the Notifications Centre: Activate or deactivate **Show On Lock Screen**.

   ➢ Activate the **Dim Lock Screen** option to darken your Lock Screen when this Focus is active

❖ After selecting the options, click the Back icon ❮ in the upper part of your display.

❖ To change the Lock Screen used when this Focus is active, touch the Lock Screen preview in the Customize Screens section, choose one of the Lock Screens, and then touch the **Done** button in the upper part of your display.

❖ To select a Home Screen page to use when this Focus is active, touch the Home Screen preview in the Customize Screens section, choose one of the pages, and then touch the **Done** button.

After you've set your Focus, you can always go back to the Settings application> Focus and change the options you selected above.

Create a Focus

If you want to focus on a task different from the available focus options, you can simply create a Focus mode.

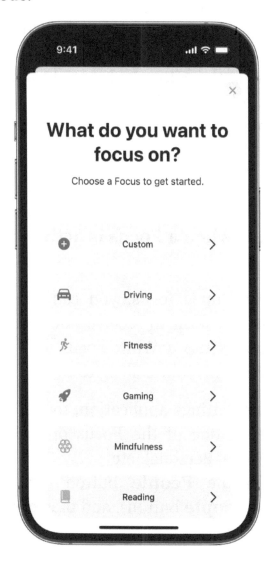

- ❖ Enter the Settings application and then tap Focus.
- ❖ Click on the Add icon➕ in the upper right corner of your display, and then click the **Custom** button.
- ❖ Give the Focus a name, and then touch the **Return** button
- ❖ Pick one of the colors and icons to represent the Focus, and then click the **Next** button.
- ❖ Click on the **Customize Focus** button, and then configure options for the Focus.

Allow or mute notifications from certain individuals when a Focus is active

When setting up a focus, you can choose which individuals you want to receive notifications from. For instance, setup a Work Focus and allow only notifications from your colleagues.

- ❖ Enter the Settings application, touch Focus, and then select one of the Focus options, such as Work, Sleep, Personal, etc.
- ❖ Click on the **People** button (or touch the **Choose People** button), and then carry out any of the below:

➢ Allow specific individuals: Touch the **Allow Notification From** button, click on the Add icon ✛, and then choose from your contacts list.

You can also activate options to allow calls from specific individuals and allow repeated calls (2 or more calls from the same individual within three minutes).

➢ Mute specific individuals: Touch the **Silence Notification From** button, click on the Add icon ✛, and then choose from your contacts list.

You can also activate the **Allow Calls From Silenced Individuals** option.

Allow or mute notifications from specific applications when a Focus is active

When setting up a focus, you can choose which applications you want to receive notifications from. For instance, setup a Work Focus and allow only notifications from applications you use for work.

❖ Enter the Settings application, touch Focus, and then select one of the Focus options, such as Work, Sleep, Personal, etc.

❖ Click on the **Apps** button (or touch the **Choose Apps** button), and then carry out any of the below:
  ➢ Allow specific applications: Touch the **Allow Notification From** button, click on the Add icon ✚ , and then choose applications.
  ➢ Mute specific applications: Touch the **Silence Notification From** button, click on the Add icon ✚ , and then choose applications.

You can also activate Time-sensitive Notifications, which allows all applications to send time-sensitive messages immediately.

Share your Focus status

When you activate a Focus, the Focus mode limits the notifications you receive from individuals & applications. If someone outside of the individuals you've allowed tries to contact you, your Focus status will appear in Messages and other applications you've given permission to, so they know you are busy.

When you allow an application to share your Focus status, other people can see that you've silenced notifications, but not the name of the focus you've activated. This info is shared only when you've activated a Focus and after you've given the application permission.

* Enter the Settings application, touch Focus, and then touch Focus Status.
* Activate Share Focus Status, and then choose the Focus options you'd like to share.

Allow calls from emergency contacts when notifications are silenced

* Enter the Contacts application
* Choose one of the contacts, and then touch the **Edit** button
* Touch Text Tone or Ringtone, and then activate the Emergency Bypass feature.
  Or, setup your Medical ID in the Health application and add emergency contacts.

Activate a Focus in the Controls Centre

* Swipe down from the upper right corner of your display to open the Controls Centre, touch the **Focus** button, and then touch the Focus you'd like to activate.

Note: If a focus is already active, it deactivates when you touch another Focus.

❖ To select an endpoint for the Focus mode, click the More Options icon, choose one of the

options (like, "Until this evening, "For an hour",
etc.), and then touch the More Options icon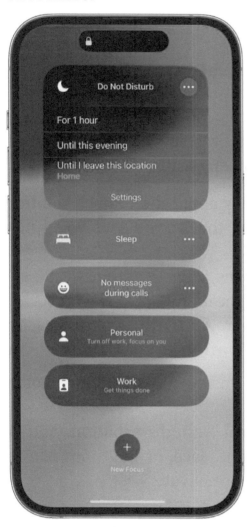
once more.

When a Focus mode is active, its icon will appear in
the status bar, and your status will be automatically

shown in the Message application. People trying to message you will see that you have temporarily turned off notifications, but they can let you know if something is urgent.

Set a Focus to activate automatically

You can set a Focus mode to activate at specific times, when you are in a specific location, or when you launch a certain application.

❖ Enter the Settings application, touch the **Focus** button, and then touch the Focus you'd like to schedule.
❖ To have this Focus activate automatically based on cues like application usage or your location, touch the **Smart Activation** button, activate the **Smart Activation** feature, and then touch the Back icon ❮ in the upper left corner of your display.
❖ Click on the **Add Schedule** button, and then set an application, place, or the times you want this Focus mode to activate.

Deactivate a Focus

❖ Carry out any of the below:
- ➢ Long-press the Focus button in your Lock Screen.
- ➢ Swipe down from the upper right corner of your display to open the Controls Centre, and then click on the **Focus** button

❖ Touch the active Focus mode to deactivate it.

Delete a Focus

❖ Enter the Settings application, and then touch Focus.

❖ Click the **Focus** button, scroll down, and then touch the **Delete** button.

Type with your iPhone keyboard

You can use your iPhone keyboard to type & edit the text in applications.

In an application that supports text editing, touch the text field to bring out your iPhone's keyboard, and then touch each button on the keyboard to type

While typing, you can carry out any of the below:

- ❖ Write Capital letters: Tap the Shift button ⇧ and then touch one of the letters.
- ❖ Activate Caps Lock: Double-touch the Shift button ⇧.
- ❖ Insert symbols, punctuations, or numbers: Touch # + = or 123

❖ Insert an emoji: Tap the Emoji button 😊 to show the emoji keyboard

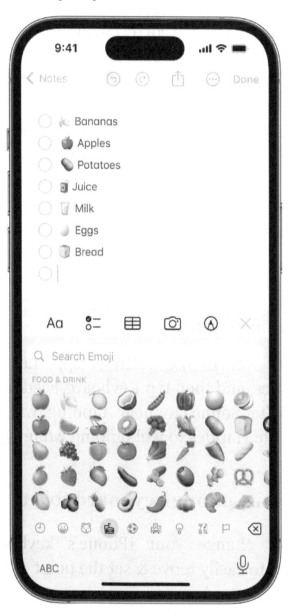

- Correct spelling: Touch a word you spelled wrongly to view suggested corrections, and then touch one of the suggestions to replace the word, or simply type the correct spelling.
- Undo the last edit: Use 3 of your fingers to swipe left, and then touch the **Undo** button on your display.
- Redo the last edit: Use 3 of your fingers to swipe right, then touch the **Redo** button.

Activate keyboard sounds & haptic feedback

Personalize keyboard settings to feel or hear tapping while typing.

- Head over to the Settings app, tap Sound & Haptics, and then tap Keyboard Feedbacks.
- Activate Sound to hear tapping while typing; activate Haptics to feel tapping while typing.

Turn your phone keyboard to a trackpad

You can change your iPhone's keyboard to a trackpad to easily move & set the point of insertion.

Slide your finger over the keyboard to move the insertion point.

❖ Use one of your fingers to long-press the Space bar till the keyboard becomes gray.
❖ Slide your finger around the keyboard to change the entry point.
To highlight text, long-press the keyboard with a 2nd finger, then move your 1st finger around the keyboard to adjust the selection.

Insert accented letters or other characters as you type

While typing on your iPhone's keyboard, long-press the symbol, number, or letter associated with the character you want to insert.

For instance, to insert **é**, long-press the **e** button, then slide your finger and lift it on the option you're looking for.

Move text

❖ In an application that allows text editing, highlight the text you'd like to move.

❖ Long-press the highlighted text till it lifts up, and then drag it to a different location in the application.

Type with one hand

You can move the keys very close to your thumb to make one-handed typing easier.

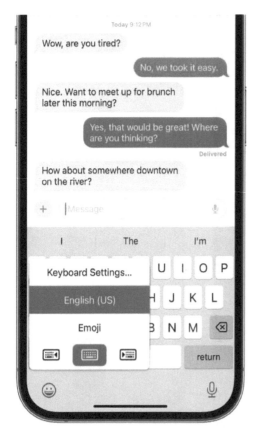

❖ Long-press the Emoji button 😃 or the Globe button 🌐

❖ Touch a keyboard layout. (For instance, touch the right-hand layout button ⌨ to move the keyboard to the right side of your display.)
To return the keyboard to its normal size, touch the left or right edge of the keyboard.

Dictation

You can dictate text anywhere you can type on your phone.

Activate Dictation

❖ Enter the Settings app, click on General, and then click on Keyboard.

❖ Activate **Enable Dictation.** If prompted, click on the **Enable Dictation** button.

Dictate text

❖ Touch to place the point of insertion when you want to enter text.

❖ Click on the Dictate button 🎙️ on your keyboard or in any field that it appears. Then start talking.

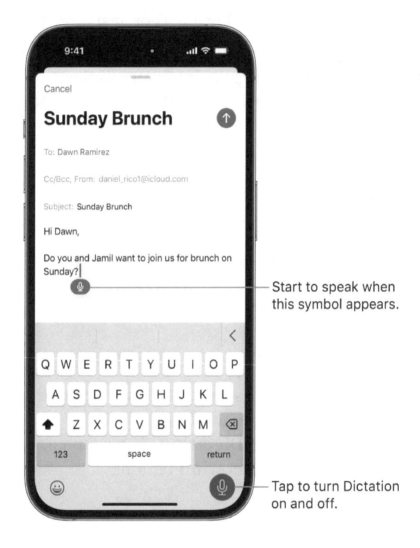

Start to speak when this symbol appears.

Tap to turn Dictation on and off.

❖ To insert a punctuation mark or an emoji while dictating, simply say the name of the emoji (for example smiley face emoji), or say the name of the punctuation mark (for example, Apostrophe)

❖ When you are done, click on the Dictation icon 🎤

Disable Dictation

❖ Head over to the Settings application, click on General, and then click Keyboard.
❖ Disable **Enable Dictation**.

Select, cut, copy & paste text

❖ Carry out any of the below to select text in a text field:
  ➢ Double-tap a word to highlight the word.
  ➢ Tap a word in a paragraph three times quickly to highlight the paragraph.
  ➢ Select a block of text: Double-tap & hold the 1st word in the text block and then drag to the last word.
❖ Once you've selected the text you'd like to edit, you can type or touch the selection to show the editing options:
  ➢ Copy: Touch the Copy button, or pinch closed with 3 of your fingers.

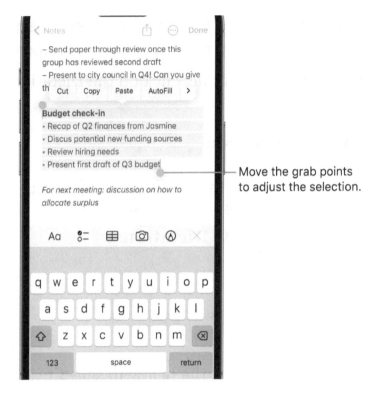

Move the grab points to adjust the selection.

➢ Cut: Click on the Cut button or use 3 fingers to pinch closed twice.
➢ Paste: Click on the **Paste** button
➢ Highlight all the text in the document: click on the **Select All** button.
➢ Format: Change the formatting of the highlighted text.
➢ Replace: Check out suggested text replacements.
➢ More Options icon ˃: See more options

Enter or edit text by typing

❖ Place the entry point where you'd like to enter or edit text by carrying out any of the below:
  ➢ Touch where you'd like to insert or edit text
  ➢ Long-press to zoom in on the text, then drag the insertion point to where you want to enter text.

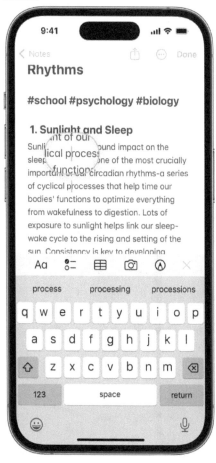

❖ Paste or type the text you want to enter.

Save keystrokes with text replacement

Create text replacements that you can use to enter phrases or words by simply typing a few letters. For instance, type "omw" to insert "On My Way".

Adhere to the instructions below to setup a text replacement:

❖ While typing with your onscreen keyboard, long-press the Globe button 🌐 or the Emoji button 😊.

❖ Touch the **Keyboard Setting** button, and then click on Text Replacements.

❖ Touch the Add button +.

❖ Type a phrase in the Phrases field, and type the shortcut in the Shortcut box.

To change a word or phrase, simply head over to the Settings app, click on **General**, click **Keyboard**, click on **Text Replacement**, click on the Add button +, and then type the phrase or word in the Phrases box, but leave the Shortcut field blank.

Switch to another keyboard

❖ While typing in a text field, long-press the Emoji button 😊 or the Globe key 🌐

❖ Touch the keyboard you'd like to switch to.

Receive government alerts

In some countries, you can activate alerts in the Government Alert list. For instance, in the US, you can receive national alerts on your device.

❖ Enter the Settings application, and then click on Notifications.
❖ Scroll to the Government Alerts segment, and then activate any of them.

Take a screenshot on your phone

You can capture what's on your iPhone's display and save it on your device, share it with other people, or add the image to documents.

❖ Press & release the side button & the Increase volume button simultaneously.

You'll see the screenshot thumbnail in the bottom left edge of your display.

❖ Touch the thumbnail to check the picture or swipe it to the left to remove it from the display.

Your Screenshots are automatically stored in the Photos application. To check out all of them in one place, launch the Photos app, touch Albums, and then touch Screenshots in the Media Types section.

Capture a full-page screenshot

You can capture a screenshot of content that's longer than the length of your screen, like an entire webpage in the Safari app.

❖ Press & release the Side button & the Increase Volume button simultaneously.
❖ Touch the screenshot's thumb-nail in the bottom left edge of your iPhone's display.
❖ Click the **Full Page** button, click on Done, and then do any of the below:
  ➢ Click on the **Save to Photos** button to store the screenshot in the Photos application
  ➢ Touch the **Save to Files** button, pick a location, and then click on the **Save** button to store the screen-shot in the Files application.

Screen recording

You can record what's happening on your iPhone's screen.

❖ Enter the Settings app, click on Controls Center, and then touch the Add icon ⊕ beside Screen Recording.

❖ Swipe-down from the upper right corner of your display to open the Controls Centre, and then click on the Screen Recording button ◉.
Your iPhone will start recording the screen after three seconds.

❖ To stop the screen recording, swipe down from the upper right corner of the screen to enter the Controls Center, click on the Stop Recording button ◎ , and then click on **Stop.**

The Screen recordings are automatically stored in the Photos application. To view all of them in one place, launch the Photos app, touch Albums, and then touch Screen Recording in the Media Types section.

Write & draw in documents with Markup

In supported applications like Photos, Notes, Message, & Mail, you can use Markup tools to draw or write in your documents, PDFs, screenshots, etc.

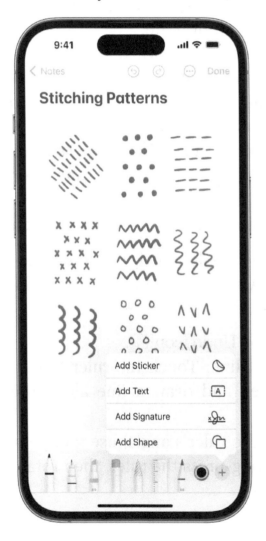

Write & draw

❖ In an application that supports Markup, click the Markup icon Ⓐ or the **Markup** button.

❖ In the Markup Tools Panel, touch one of the tools, like the pencil, marker, or pen, and then use your finger to draw or write.

Do any of the below while drawing:

➢ Change the weight of a line: Touch the selected drawing tool in the Tools panel, and then touch one of the options.

➢ Change the transparency: Touch the selected drawing tool in the Tools panel, and then slide the slider.

➢ Change the colour: Click the Colour Picker button ● in the Tools panel, and then click on Spectrum, Grid, or Sliders to adjust the colour selection.

➢ Undo: Touch the Undo icon ↺.

➢ Draw a straight line: Touch the ruler tool in the Tools panel, and draw a line along the ruler's edge.

• To change the ruler's angle, use 2 of your fingers to long-press the ruler, then rotate your fingers

- Use one of your fingers to drag the ruler to move it without changing its angle.
- To hide the ruler, simply touch the ruler tool in the Tools panel once more

❖ Click on the Markup icon ⊚ or the **Done** button to close the Markup Tools panel.

Erase an error

In the application you're using, click the eraser tool in the Markup Tools panel, and then carry out any of the below:

❖ Erase with Pixel Eraser: Use one of your fingers to scrub over the mistake.
❖ Erase with the object eraser: Use one of your fingers to touch the object.
❖ Switch between object & pixel erasing tools: Touch the Eraser tool once more in the Tools panel, and then touch Object Eraser or Pixel Eraser.

Magnify items around you

In the Magnifier application, you can use your phone to zoom in on items close to you.

❖ Launch the Magnifier application

❖ Drag the slider to the right or left to adjust the zoom level.
❖ Use any of the controls below:
  ➢ Click on the Contrast button ◖ to change the contrast level
  ➢ Click on the Brightness button ☀ to change the brightness level.
  ➢ Click the Flashlight button ⵊ to turn on the flashlight.
  ➢ Tap on the Filters button ⊕ to apply colour filters.
  ➢ Click on the Camera icon 📷 to switch to the back or the front-facing camera.
  ➢ Touch the Lock button 🔒 to lock the focus
  ➢ Touch the Freeze icon ◉ to freeze the frame
  ➢ To freeze more frames, touch the Multi-Photos Mode icon ⧉, and then click on the Add icon ⊕
  To view the frames, touch the **View** button, and then touch the frames you'd like to see. Click on the **Done** button or the Cancel icon ⊗ to go back to the live lens.

Create playlists on your phone

In the Music application, you can create a playlist &
add songs that you can share with others.

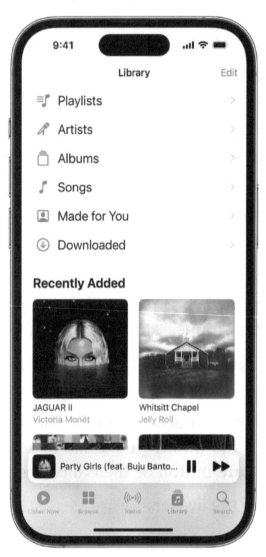

Create a playlist

❖ To create a playlist in the Music app, touch the **Library** button, click on the **Playlist** button, and then touch the **New Playlist** button.

❖ Type a name & description to make it easy to identify the playlist.
❖ To give the playlist a cover art, touch the Camera button, and then capture a picture or pick one of the pictures from your Photos Library.

❖ Touch the **Create** button, and then touch the **Add Music** button

You can choose music from your library, search for songs, or select songs listed in the lower part of your display.

❖ Click on the Add icon ⊕ to add the song to your playlist.

The Music application recommends songs for the playlist you create. To add any of the suggested songs to a playlist, simply swipe to the bottom of your display, and then touch the Add icon ⊕ beside the song. Touch the Refresh icon ↻ to refresh the suggestions list.

If you want songs to be added to your library when you add them to any of your playlists, enter the Settings application, touch Music, and then activate **Add Playlist Song**.

Edit your playlist

Touch the playlist, touch the More Options icon ⊙, touch the **Edit** button, and then carry out any of the below:

❖ Add songs: Touch the **Add Music** button, and then select songs.
Or, long-press an item (playlist, music video, album, or song), click on the **Add to a Playlist** button, and then choose one of the playlists.

❖ Delete a song: Touch the Delete icon⬤, and then touch the **Delete** button. Removing a song from your playlist does not remove the song from your music library

❖ Rearrange the songs: Drag the Reorder button ☰ beside a song.

❖ Edit cover art: Choose from the different Apple templates to use as your playlist cover art.

Sort your playlist

❖ Tap one of your playlists, and then touch the More Options icon⊙ in the upper right part of your display.

❖ Touch the **Sort By** button, and then pick one of the options.

Delete a playlist

Long-press the playlist and then touch the **Delete from Library** button.

Or, click the playlist, touch the More Options icon ⊙, and then click the **Delete from Library** button

AirDrop

You can use AirDrop to wirelessly send videos, locations, sites, pictures, etc. to other Apple devices that are close to your iPhone.

AirDrop moves data over WiFi & Bluetooth, so both must be activated. You must log in with your Apple ID to use AirDrop.

You can reject or accept requests as they arrive.

Send something via AirDrop

❖ Open the item you want to send on your phone, and then click the More Options icon •••, the Share icon ⬆, the **Share** button, the **AirDrop** button, or any other button that shows the application's sharing options.

❖ Click the AirDrop icon ⊚, and then touch the AirDrop user you want to send the item to.

If the individual does not appear on your phone as an AirDrop user, tell the person to open the Controls Centre on their device & let AirDrop receive items. If you want to send an item to a Mac user, tell the individual to allow themselves to be discovered in AirDrop in the Finder.

Control who can
send items to you.

Let others send things to your phone via AirDrop

❖ Swipe down from the upper right corner of your display to show the Controls Centre, long-press the upper-left set of controls, and then click on the AirDrop icon .

❖ Click on **Everybody for Ten Minutes** or **Only Contacts** to select who you'd like to get items from.

Use Guided Access

The Guided Access feature helps you focus on a task by temporarily restricting your phone to an application and letting you control which application features are available. You can:

- ❖ Limit how long a person can use the application
- ❖ Deactivate your phone hardware buttons
- ❖ Turn off areas of your display that are not relevant to your task, or areas that may cause a distraction when it's touched accidentally

Setup Guided Access

- ❖ Enter the Settings application, touch Accessibility, touch Guided Access, and then activate the **Guided Access** feature.

‹ Back **Guided Access**

Guided Access

Guided Access keeps the iPhone in a single app, and allows you to control which features are available. To start Guided Access, triple-click the side button in the app you want to use.

Passcode Settings ›

- ❖ Make adjustments to any of the below:

> Passcode Setting: Click on the **Set Guided Access Passcode** button and then insert a password.
You can also activate Face ID as a means to end a Guided Access session.
> Accessibility Shortcuts: Activate or deactivate the shortcut during Guided Access session
> Time Limits: Play a sound or have the remaining Guided Access time spoken before a session ends.
> Display Auto-Lock: Set how long it will take your device to automatically lock when Guided Access is activated.

Start a Guided Access session

❖ Launch the application you want to use.
❖ Swipe down from the upper right corner of your display to open the Controls Centre, and then touch the **Guided Access** button 🔒
(If you can't find the Guided Access button in the Controls Centre, you can add it—simply enter the Settings application, touch Controls Centre, and then click on the Add icon ➕ beside Guided Access.)

❖ Use one of your fingers to circle where you want to disable on your iPhone's screen. Move the circle or use the handles to change the size, or touch the **X** button to remove it.

❖ Touch Options, and then activate or deactivate any of the below:

- ➢ Touch
- ➢ Keyboards
- ➢ Volume Buttons
- ➢ Side Button
- ➢ Time Limit
- ➢ Motion(to stop your phone from switching to portrait to landscape orientation or from responding to any other motion)
- ❖ Touch the **Start** button.

Please note: Emergency Services & Crash Detection aren't available when Guided Access is active. You'll have to end the **Guided Access** session first before you can make emergency calls or use the Crash Detection feature.

End a Guided Access session

Carry out any of the below:

- ❖ Use the Guided Access password: Press the Side button three times quickly, and then insert the Guided Access passcode.
- ❖ Use the **Face ID** feature: Press the side button twice quickly, and then stare at your display to unlock with Face ID.

Make text more legible on your device

You can adjust the darkness level, size, & weight of the text in applications that support Dynamic Type (like Notes, Message, Mail, Contacts, Calendar, & Settings). You can also make your phone underline text you can touch/tap.

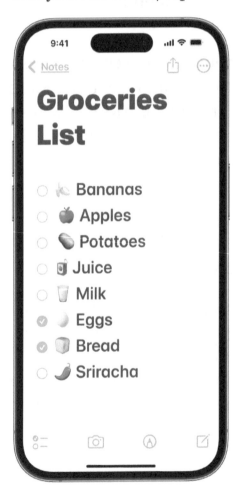

❖ Enter the Settings application, touch Accessibility, and then touch Display & Text Size.
❖ Carry out any of the below:
  ➤ Increase the size of text: Touch the **Larger Text** button, and then drag the slider to change the size of text on your display (activate the **Larger Accessibility Sizes** feature to see more size options).
  ➤ Activate **Bold Text** to make the text on your screen heavier
  ➤ Increase the darkness level of text: Activate **Increase Contrast** to make text stand out and increase legibility.
  ➤ Identify text that can be tapped: Activate **Button Shapes** to underline texts that perform actions when you touch them.

Change the text size when using an application

❖ Swipe down from the upper right corner of your display to open the Controls Center, and then touch the Text Size button AA.

(If you can't find the Text Size button A A in the Controls Centre, you can add it—simply enter the Settings application, touch Controls Centre, and then click on the Add icon ⊕ beside Text Size.)

❖ Drag the slider down or up to change the text size.

To adjust the text size for all applications, click on the **All Apps** button in the lower part of your display.

Adjust settings for your iPhone's Side button

❖ Enter the Settings application, touch Accessibility, and then touch Side Button.
❖ Set any of the below:
  ➢ Click Speed: Select the speed required to triple-click or double-click the side button.
  ➢ Press & Hold to Speak: Choose whether Siri will respond when you long-press the side button.

Set the on-screen keyboard to show only uppercase letters

If you have trouble seeing the keyboard on your screen, you can set the keyboard to show only capital letters.

Enter the Settings application, touch Accessibility, touch Keyboards, and then deactivate **Show Lowercase Keys**.

Type on a bigger on-screen keyboard

Rotate your phone to landscape orientation to use the larger keyboard to type in many applications, including Contacts, Notes, Messages, Safari, & Mail.

Control nearby Apple devices with your iPhone

You can use your phone to remotely control other Apple devices.

❖ Enter the Settings application, touch Accessibility, touch Control Nearby Device, and then click on Control Nearby Device.

The device you'd like to control needs to be using the same Apple ID and connected to the same WiFi network as your iPhone.

❖ Select the device from the list, and then touch one of the buttons.

The name of the buttons corresponds to the controls on your device. Click on the More Options icon⊙ to show more options.

Touch the Close button × to stop controlling the other Apple device.

Recognize sound with your iPhone

Your iPhone can constantly listen for certain sounds—like a crying baby, siren, or doorbells—and alert you when it detects these sounds.

Please note: Do not rely on your phone to recognize sound in situations that could cause injury or harm to you, in emergencies or high-risk situations, or for navigation.

Setup Sound Recognition

❖ Enter the Settings application, touch Accessibility, touch Sound Recognition, and then activate Sounds Recognition.

❖ Click on the **Sounds** button, and then activate the sounds you want your device to recognize.

Add custom alarms, doorbells, or appliances

Set your phone to recognize a specific doorbell, appliance, or alarm if it doesn't recognize them automatically.

❖ Enter the Settings application, touch Accessibility, touch Sound Recognition, and then touch Sounds.
❖ Touch Custom Doorbell or Appliance or Custom Alarm, and then type a name
❖ When the doorbell, appliance, or alarm is ready, place your phone close to the sound and ensure there's no other sound playing around your iPhone at that moment.
❖ Touch the **Start Listening** button, and then adhere to the directives on your screen.

Flash the LED for alerts on your phone

You can set your phone to flash the LED that's close to the back camera lens when someone calls you or when you receive other alerts.

❖ Enter the Settings application, touch Accessibility, touch Audio/Visuals, and then activate **LED Flash for Alerts**.
❖ Deactivate **Flash on Silent** to stop the LED from flashing when Silent mode is activated
❖ Activate **Flash While Unlock** to allow flashlight alerts when your phone is unlocked.

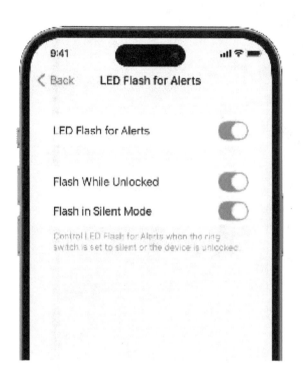

Get Live Captions in real-time on your phone

The Live Captions feature allows your phone to turn spoken dialogue into text and show it on your iPhone screen in real time. You can easily follow the audio in an application, like Podcasts or Face-Time, and in conversations around you.

Setup & personalize Live Captions

❖ Enter the Settings application, touch Accessibility, and then touch Live Captions.
❖ Activate Live Captions, and then touch the **Appearance** button to personalize the caption's size, text, and colour.
❖ By default, Live Captions are displayed across all applications. To get Live Captions for some applications, like RTT or Face-Time, activate them in the **In-Apps Live Captions** section.

See live captions

The Live Captions feature allows your iPhone to automatically transcribe the dialogue around you or in applications. With Live Captions activated, you can carry out any of the below:

❖ Transcribe a conversation close to you: Click the Microphone icon 🎤 .
❖ Increase the size of the transcription window: Click the Maximize icon 🔳. Click the Minimize icon 🔳 to return the window to a smaller size.
❖ Click on the Pause icon ⏸ to pause the transcription

❖ Hide the transcription window: Click the Collapse icon ⬤. Click the Restore Live Captions button ⬤ to restore the window.

Play soothing sounds on your phone to block out noise around you

You can play soothing sounds on your phone to mask unwanted environmental noise and reduce distractions so that you can rest or focus on a task.

❖ Enter the Settings application, touch Accessibility, touch Audio/Visual, touch Background Sound, and then activate Background Sound.
❖ Set any of the below:
  ➢ Sound: Select one of the sounds; the file will download to your phone.
  ➢ Volume: Drag the slider to the right or left.
  ➢ Use while media is playing: Change the volume of background sound when your phone is playing music or other media.
  ➢ Mute sound when locked: Background sound will stop playing when your phone is locked.

Listen to your phone speak the screen, highlighted text, & typing feed-back

You can have your phone speak highlighted text or the whole screen.

Select a style for spoken content

❖ Head over to the Settings app, click on Accessibility, and then click Spoken Content.
❖ Activate any of the below:
  ➢ Speak Selection: Highlight the text you want to be read out.
  ➢ Speak Screen: Have your phone read out everything on your screen.
  ➢ Speech control: Display the Speech controller for easy access to the Speak Screen.
  ➢ Highlight content: Your phone can highlight words as they are spoken.
  ➢ Typing Feedback: You can set typing feedback for your keyboard and choose to have your phone read out each character, whole words, auto-caps, etc.
    To hear typing predictions, you also have to enter the Settings app, touch General, touch Keyboards, and then activate **Predictive**.

- ➢ Voice: Pick one of the voices & accents.
- ➢ Slide the slider to set the speaking rate
- ➢ Pronunciation: Dictate or spell how you want your iPhone to pronounce certain sentences.

Hear your phone speak

You can summon Siri and then say "Speak Screen".

You could say "Hey Siri Speak Screen"

Or carry out any of the below:

- ❖ Hear highlighted text: select a word or paragraph, and then touch the **Speak** button.
- ❖ Hear the whole screen: Use 2 of your fingers to swipe down from the upper edge of your screen. Use the visual controls to pause the speech or adjust the speed.
- ❖ Hear typing feed-back: Start typing. Long-press each word to hear typing predictions (when activated).

Back Tap

The Back Tap feature allows your phone to perform a specific action—like capturing a screenshot, activating an accessibility feature, etc.—when you triple-tap or double-tap the back of your phone

- ❖ Enter the Settings app, click Accessibility, tap **Touch**, and then click Back Tap.
- ❖ Touch Triple-Tap or Double-Tap, and then pick one of the actions.
- ❖ Triple-tap or double-tap the back of your phone to perform the action you've set.

To disable the Back Tap feature, enter the Settings app, click Accessibility, tap **Touch**, click Back Tap, touch Double Tap or Triple Tap, and then click on the **None** option.

Turn off all vibrations on your phone

Enter the Settings app, click on Accessibility, tap **Touch**, and then deactivate Vibration

Reachability

With the **Reachability** feature, you can lower the top half of your display so that you can easily reach it with your thumb.

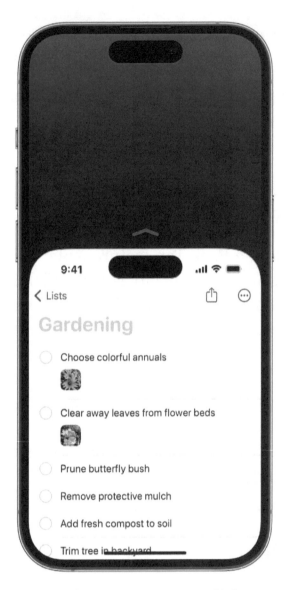

❖ Head over to the Settings app, click Accessibility, tap **Touch**, and then enable the **Reachability** feature.

❖ Swipe down from the lower edge of your display to lower the upper half of your display.

❖ Touch the top half of your display to go back to full screen.

Use your device as a remote microphone

The Live Listen feature allows you to stream sound from the MIC on your phone to your AirPods or other hearing devices. This can be very helpful when you are discussing in a noisy place.

❖ Connect your AirPods to your phone and put them on your ears.
❖ Do any of the below to enable or disable the Live Listen feature:
  ➢ Swipe down from the upper right corner of your display to open the Controls Centre, click on the Hearing Devices button, touch your AirPods or a hearing device, and then touch the **Live Listen** button.
    (If you cannot find the Hearing Devices icon in the Controls Center, you can add it—simply head over to the Settings app, click on Controls Centre, and then touch the Add icon ⊕ close to Hearing.)
  ➢ If you are making use of a hearing aid, head over to the Settings application, touch Accessibility, click on Hearing Devices, and then enable the **Live Listen** feature.
❖ Place your phone very close to the sound source.

Type-to-speak with Live Speech

The Live Speech feature allows you to type & have your words spoken in person & on calls

❖ Enter the Settings app, click on Accessibility, click Live Speech, and then enable Live Speech.
❖ Choose one of the voices.
❖ Press the side button three times quickly, enter text in the text field, and then click on the **Send** button to have your text read out.

People will hear your words spoken in the conversation if you are making use of the Phone or Face-Time application. Otherwise, they'll come out of your iPhone's speakers.

Record your Personal Voice

With the **Personal Voice** feature, you can create a voice that sounds just like yours and use it in FaceTime & Phone calls, and some applications

❖ Enter the Settings app, touch Accessibility, and then touch Personal Voice.
❖ Click on the **Create Personal Voice** button, and then follow the prompts.
   (If you want to pause the recording session, simply touch the **Done** button. Touch the **Continue Recording** button to continue.)

Your Personal Voice is safely stored on your phone for use in Phone & Face-Time calls, private chats, and some 3rd-party applications.

Customize the sharing options in apps on your phone

You can pick the options that appear in an application's Sharing menu and rearrange them too.

❖ Open a document in the application, and then touch the Share icon⬆️

❖ Swipe left on the row of buttons, touch the **More** button, and then click on the **Edit** button.

❖ Carry out any of the below:

 ➢ Show options: Touch to enable the option

 ➢ Hide options: Touch to disable the option.

 ➢ Add options to Favourites: Touch the Add icon➕ next to the option.

 ➢ Remove options from Favourites: Touch the Remove icon➖ next to the option.

 ➢ Reorder options in Favourites by dragging the Rearrange icon☰ beside an option to another position.

❖ Touch the **Done** button.

PERSONALIZE THE LOCK SCREEN

You can customize the Lock Screen by picking a wallpaper, displaying a favourite picture, changing the time's font, etc.

Customize a new Lock Screen

❖ Long-press the Lock Screen till you see the **Customize** button & the Add icon ⊕ in the lower part of your screen.
If they do not appear, long-press the Lock Screen once more, and then insert your password.

❖ Click on the Add icon  to create a new lock screen, or change some things in a Lock Screen, swipe to the screen you'd like to edit, touch the **Customize** button, and then touch the **Lock Screen** button.

❖ If you want to create a new Lock Screen, touch any of the wallpapers to choose it as your Lock Screen.

❖ Touch the time to change its colour, style, & font. Drag the slider to the left or right to make the font lighter or thicker.

❖ To add widgets that have info like weather reports, or today's headline, just click on the

Add Widgets button, the date, or the box under the time.

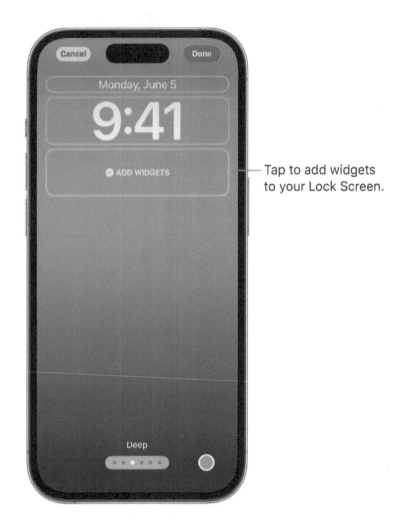

Tap to add widgets to your Lock Screen.

❖ Touch the **Done** button or the **Add** button, and then click on the **Set as Wallpaper Pair** button or the **Customize Home Screen** button.

➢ Touch the **Set as Wallpaper Pair** button to use the wallpaper on your Lock & Home Screen.
➢ Make more adjustments to the Home Screen: Touch the **Customize Home Screen** option. Touch one of the colors to change the colour of the wallpaper, click the Pictures icon to use one of your pictures, or touch the **Blur** button to blur the wallpaper

Personalize your Lock Screen photo

If you select a picture for your Lock Screen, you can customize it to fit your style.

Do any of the below:

❖ Reposition the picture: To change the position of the picture you've selected, pinch open to zoom in on the picture, use 2 fingers to drag the picture around, and then pinch closed to zoom out.
❖ Use a different style for the photo: Swipe right or left to check out different photos style with additional colour filters & fonts.

❖ Create a multi-layered effect: If the picture is compatible with layering—like a picture with animals, people, or the sky/clouds— touch the More Options button⊙ in the lower right part of your screen, and then click the **Depth Effects** button.

❖ Create motion effects with Live Photos: If you selected a Live Photo that can be played in slow motion, tap the Play icon▶ in the lower part of your screen to play the Live Photo anytime you wake your iPhone.

❖ Set the switching frequency: If you select the Photos Shuffle option, you can browse the pictures by touching the Browse icon▦, and you can set the shuffle frequency by clicking the More Options button⊙, and then choosing one of the options under Shuffle Frequency.

Tip: You can also add a picture directly from the Photos application to your Lock Screen & Home Screen. In the Photos application, click on the **Library** tab, select one of the photos, and then tap the Share icon⬆. Scroll down, touch the **Use as Wallpaper** button, click on the **Add** button, and then touch the **Set as Wallpaper Pair** option to use the wallpaper on your Lock and Home Screens.

Link a Focus to your Lock Screen

The Focus feature helps iPhone users to focus their attention on a task by reducing distractions. You can setup a Focus to temporarily mute all notifications/alerts or allow only certain alerts/notifications (for instance, notifications related to the task you're working on). When you link a Focus to your Lock Screen, the Focus Setting will activate anytime you make use of that Lock Screen.

❖ Long-press the Lock Screen till you see the **Customize** button on your screen.
❖ Touch the Focus button in the lower part of the wallpaper to view the Focus modes—for instance, Work, Sleep, & DND.

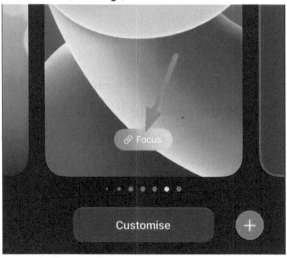

❖ Select one of the Focus options, and then click the Close icon ✕ .

Customize or change your Lock Screen

After creating a custom Lock Screen, you can edit it.

❖ Long-press the Lock Screen till you see the **Customize** button & the Add icon ⊕ on your display.
If they do not appear, long-press the Lock Screen once more, and then insert your password.

❖ Swipe to the lock screen you'd like to edit, touch the **Customize** button, and then click the **Lock Screen** option.

❖ Touch the time to use another colour, style, & font.

❖ To add widgets, simply touch the **Add Widgets** button, the date, or the box under the time.

❖ Touch the **Done** button or the **Add** button, and then click on the **Set as Wallpaper Pair** or the **Customize Home Screen** button.

Move from one Lock Screen to another

You can create multiple Lock Screens and then move from one to another anytime you like

❖ Long-press the Lock Screen till you see the **Customize** button on your screen.
❖ Swipe to the Lock Screen you'd like to use, and then touch it.

Delete a Lock Screen

❖ Long-press the Lock Screen till you see the **Customize** button on your screen.
❖ Swipe to the Lock Screen you'd like to remove from your device, swipe up on the Lock Screen, touch the Delete icon 🗑, and then touch the **Delete This Wallpaper** button.

INTERACT WITH TEXT & SUBJECTS IN PICTURES

Live Text

When viewing a picture or when you Pause a video in the Photos application, Live Text identifies the text & info in the picture, allowing you to interact with it in many ways. You can highlight text to translate, share, copy, and more.

Activate Live Text

Before you use Live Text, ensure you've activated it for all supported languages.

❖ Head over to the Settings app, touch General, and then click Language & Region.
❖ Activate the **Live Text** feature.

Use Live Text

❖ Open a picture or pause a movie that has text in it.

❖ Touch the Live Text icon, and then long-press the highlighted text.

❖ Select the text you want using the grab points, and then carry out any of the below:
  ➢ Copy text.
  ➢ Tap the **Select All** button to select every text in the frame.
  ➢ Tap the **Translate** button to translate the text you've selected.
  ➢ Tap the **Lookup** button to see specific website suggestions.
  ➢ Search the web: Get more information about the selected text on the internet.
  ➢ Tap the **Share** button to share text using one of the sharing options.
❖ Click on the End Live Text icon to go back to the video or picture.

Perform a task within a video or picture

Depending on what is in the video or picture, you can touch one of the quick actions in the lower part of your iPhone's display to do things like convert currencies, translate languages, receive directions, make a call, etc.

❖ In the Photos application, open an image or pause a movie that has text in it.

* Tap the Live Text button
* Click on one of the quick actions in the lower part of your screen.

* Click on the End Live Text icon to go back to the video or picture.

Visual Look Up

Use the **Visual Lookup** feature to identify objects in a picture and get more info about famous places, animals, plants, etc.

Visual Look Up
is available.

❖ Open a picture or pause a video.

If you see the Info icon ⊕ or ⊕ on your iPhone's screen, it means Visual Lookup is available.

❖ Touch the Visual Lookup icon, and then touch Lookup in the upper part of the picture info to see the Visual Look Up results.

❖ Touch the Close button × to close the Visual Lookup results, then swipe down on the video frame or picture to close the photo info.

Isolate a subject from the video or picture background

In the Photo application, you can remove the subject of a video or picture from its background, and then share or copy it.

❖ Open a picture or pause a video.
❖ Long-press the subject. Do any of the below when you see an outline around the subject:
  ➢ Keep tapping the subject, and then open a document in another application with another finger & drag the subject into the document.

➢ Touch the Copy button, and then paste the subject into a note, text message, or email.

- ➢ Touch the **Lookup** button to see results & get more information about the subject.
- ➢ Touch the **Add Stickers** button, and then store the sticker for use in pictures, e-mails, messages, etc.
- ➢ Touch the **Share** button, and then choose one of the sharing options.

SIRI

With Siri's help, you can perform tasks on your iPhone using your voice. You can use Siri to get weather reports, find locations, set alarms, translate a sentence, etc.

Siri responds to a request for an alarm at 8:00 AM.

Indicates that Siri is listening.

Setup Siri

If you did not setup Siri when setting up your phone, simply carry out any of the below:

❖ If you would like to use your voice to activate Siri: Enter the Settings app, click Siri & Search, touch the "Listen For" button, and then select "Siri" or "Hey Siri"
❖ If you would like to use a button to activate Siri: Enter the Settings app, click on Siri & Search, and then enable Press Side Button for Siri.

Activate Siri

Long-press the Side button or say "Hey Siri" or "Siri" and then make a request or ask a question.

For instance, you could say "Hey Siri, what is the weather report for tomorrow?"

Type instead of talking to Siri

❖ Enter the Settings app, click Accessibility, click Siri, and then enable the **Type to Siri** feature.

- To make a request, summon Siri, and then type your request in the text field

Tell Siri about yourself

For a more personalized experience, you can give Siri info, including your relationship details, and your work & home address, so you can say things like "Give me directions to my house" & "FaceTime dad."

Tell Siri who you are

- Launch the Contacts app, click on **My Cards** in the upper part of your screen, click on the **Edit** button, and then fill in your contact info.
- Head over to the Settings app, touch Siri & Search, click on My Information, and then touch your name.

Tell Siri about a relationship

You could say "Hey Siri, Herbert Clark is my husband" or "Siri, James Damian is my father"

Announce calls

With the Announce Call feature, Siri can identify an incoming Face-Time or phone call, which you can use your voice to decline or accept.

❖ Enter the Settings app, click on Siri & Search, click Announce Calls, and then choose one of the options.
❖ When someone calls your phone, Siri will identify the caller, and ask if you would like to take the call. Say **Yes** to accept the call or **No** to reject it.

Change when Siri responds

Enter the Settings app, touch Siri & Search, and then do any of the below:

❖ Disable the **Listen for "Hey Siri"** feature to stop your phone from responding to the "Hey Siri" voice request.
❖ Disable the **Press Side Button for Siri** feature to stop Siri from responding to the side button.

- ❖ Disable the **Allow Siri When Locked** feature to disable access to Siri when your phone is locked.
- ❖ Change the language Siri responds to: Click on the **Language** button, and then select one of the languages.

Change Siri's voice

- ❖ Enter the Settings app, and then touch Siri & Search.
- ❖ Click on Siri Voice, and then choose one of the voices.

Change how Siri responds

Enter the Settings app, touch Siri & Search, and then carry out any of the below:

- ❖ View your request on the screen: Click on **Siri's Response**, and then activate **Always Show Speech**
- ❖ Always show Siri's response on your iPhone screen: Click on Siri Response, and then activate Always Show Siri Captions

❖ Change when Siri responds by voice: Touch Siri
Responses, and then choose one of the options
under Spoken Response.

SAFETY FEATURES

Use Emergency SOS via satellite

You can contact emergency services via satellite if you don't have mobile or WiFi coverage.

Before disconnecting from mobile networks & WiFi

If you are traveling to a location that may not have WiFi & cellular coverage, setup your Medical ID, add emergency contacts, and then try the Emergency SOS demo before you leave.

* Enter the Settings app, and click on Emergency SOS.
* Scroll down and click on the **Try Demo** button.

Connect to Emergency SOS via satellite

You can use Emergency SOS via satellite to contact emergency services if you are in a location that doesn't have a WiFi or mobile connection.

❖ Call 911 or any other emergency service number you know. Even if you do not have a regular cellular network, your phone will try to call 911 through another network.

❖ If it does not go through, click on the **Emergency Text via Satellite** button to text the emergency department. Or, enter the Message application and text 911 or SOS, and then touch the **Emergency Services** button

❖ Touch the **Report Emergency** button and then adhere to the directives on your display.

Important: To connect to a satellite, simply hold your iPhone in your hand—you do not need to raise your iPhone up, just ensure your phone is facing the sky. If you are surrounded by thick foliage or other obstacles, you may not be able to connect to a satellite.

After connecting to a satellite, your phone will start a text conversation by sharing important info like your Medical ID & emergency contact info (if you've set them up), your answers to the emergency questions, your location, and the battery level of your phone.

Ask for roadside assistance via satellite

If you have car trouble while in a location that doesn't have mobile or WiFi coverage, you can request Roadside Assistance via satellite.

Get roadside assistance via satellite

❖ Launch the Message application on your phone.

❖ Touch the Compose icon  , and then type **"roadside"** in the address box.

❖ Click on the **Roadside Assistance** button, and then adhere to the guidelines on your screen.

Important: To connect to a satellite, simply hold your iPhone in your hand—you do not need to raise your iPhone up, just ensure it is facing the sky. If you are surrounded by thick foliage or other obstacles, you may not be able to connect to the satellite.

After connecting your phone to the satellite, you will be asked for important info, like your car's model, and the problem your car is having. They will also ask if you are already a AAA(American Automobile Association) member, so please ensure you have your AAA info with you. If you aren't a AAA member, you can still receive help.

After answering the questions, you will be told how to connect to a satellite and you will be able to communicate directly with the roadside assistance provider. They may ask you some follow-up questions to ensure they send you the right help. You can contact them with any questions about how long it will take for someone to arrive and how much the service will cost.

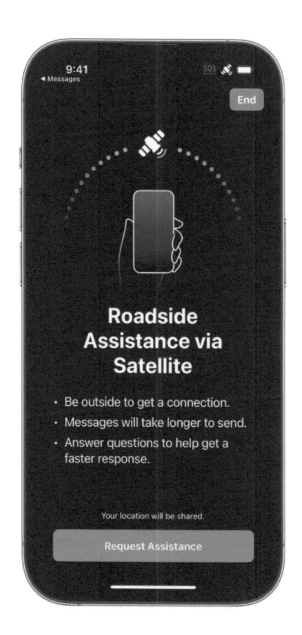

Create & view your medical ID

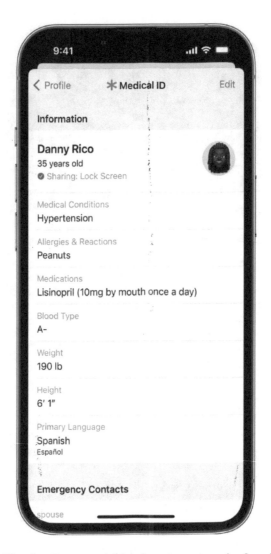

Your Medical ID provides important info about you that might be useful in emergency situations, such as your emergency contact info, allergies, and more. Your phone can provide this info to the person attending to you in an emergency situation.

Set up your medical ID

Setup a Medical ID in the Health application.

❖ Enter the Health application.
❖ Touch your photo or your initials in the upper right part of your iPhone's screen, and then touch the **Medical ID** button
❖ Touch the **Get Started** button or the **Edit** button, and then fill in your details.
❖ In the Emergency Contact section, click the **Add Emergency Contact** button, and then add the contacts
   After ending an emergency call, your device will alert your emergency contacts via text message unless you decide to cancel. Your phone will also send your location details to your emergency contacts.
❖ Click the **Done** button.

Tip: To see your Medical ID from your iPhone's Home screen, long-press the Health application's icon, and then touch the **Medical ID** option.

Let emergency services & first responders gain access to your Medical information

❖ Enter the Health application.
❖ Click your photo or your initials in the upper right corner of your iPhone's screen, and then touch the **Medical ID** button.
❖ Touch the **Edit** button, scroll down, and then activate the **Show When Locked & Emergency Call** feature.

Note: First responders can find your Medical ID from your iPhone's Lock Screen by swiping up, touching the **Emergency** button in the passcode display, and then clicking the **Medical ID** button.

Use Check-In to let your friends know that you have arrived

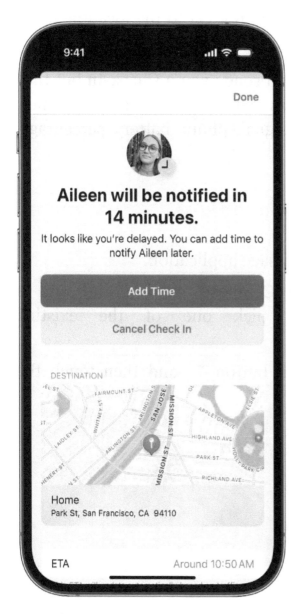

The **Check-In** feature allows your phone to notify a friend when you arrive at a specified location at a set time. You can also choose which information they can see if you do not get to the location at the time you set.

Likewise, if a friend sends you a Check-In but they haven't arrived as expected, you can see their location, mobile signal, phone battery percentage, etc.

Send a Check In

❖ Launch the Message application.

❖ Click on the Compose icon ☑ and add a recipient, or pick one of the existing conversations.

❖ Touch the Add button ✛ , and then touch the **More** button

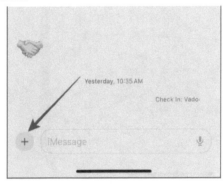

❖ Touch the **Check In** button, and then touch the **Edit** button.

❖ Select any of the below:

> **When I Arrive:** Specify where you are going, how you are going (drive, bus, or walk), and add more time if needed. The **Check-In** feature will monitor your journey and notify your friend if your phone is inactive for a long time or if you do not arrive at your expected destination. When you arrive safely at your destination, Check-In is completed automatically and your friend will

receive a notification that you have arrived at your destination.

➤ **After the timer:** Set a time—for instance, if you are meeting someone for the first time. If you do not end the Check-In before the scheduled time, Check-In will send your friend a notification.

❖ Touch the send icon ⬆.
If your phone does not get to your destination or you do not cancel Check-In, and you do not respond to Check-In messages, your phone's journey info will be sent to your friend.

Add more time to your Check-In

If you need more time, simply adhere to the directives below to add time to your Check-In:

❖ Launch the Messages application.
❖ Open the conversation with the individual you sent a Check-In to.
❖ In the Check In message, touch the **Details** button, click on the **Add Time** button, and then choose an option.

Cancel a Check In

If you complete your journey or want to end the session, you can cancel your Check-In message.

❖ Launch the Message application.
❖ Open the conversation with the individual you sent a Check-In to.

❖ In the Check-In message, touch the **Details** button, then click the **Cancel Check-In** button

Choose what information you share

You can change the info you share with your friend when a Check-In is active

❖ Enter the Settings app, and touch Messages.
❖ Scroll down and then touch the **Check-In Data** button
❖ Select the information you'd like to share if you do not finish your Check-In as expected:
  ➢ Limited: Share your location plus battery percentage & network signal.
  ➢ Full: Share the above info (network signal, current location, & battery information) in addition to your journey and the last time you unlocked your phone.

Crash Detection

If a serious car accident is detected by your iPhone, it can help you contact the emergency department & inform your emergency contacts about your situation.

How Crash Detection Function

If your smartphone detects a serious accident in your car, it'll show a notification and automatically start calling emergency services after twenty seconds if it's not canceled. If you're unresponsive, your smartphone will play a voice message for the emergency department, informing them that you have been in an accident & and giving them your location details.

If you are involved in a severe car accident & unresponsive in a place that doesn't have a mobile or WiFi connection, your phone will try to contact the emergency department using Emergency SOS via satellite if possible.

Activate or disable Crash Detection

Crash Detection is enabled by default. To disable it, simply enter the Settings app, touch Emergency SOS, and then disable the **Call after Severe Crash** feature.

Safety Check

The Safety Check feature allows you to quickly stop sharing your phone access & personal details with other people. This feature helps iPhone users to quickly change their phone passcode & Apple ID login code, stop sharing their location via Find My, etc.

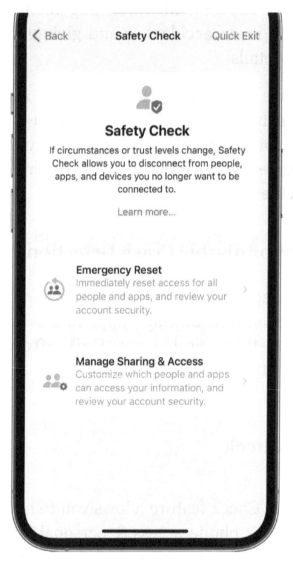

❖ Enter the Setting application, touch Privacy and Security, and then touch Safety Check.

❖ Touch the **Emergency Reset** button, touch **Start Emergency Reset**, and then adhere to the guidelines on the screen

With the Safety Check feature, you can also periodically review & make changes to the details you share with other devices, applications, & individuals.

SCREEN TIME

The Screen Time feature gives you info about how you & members of your family spend time on your Apple devices, including the applications and sites you use and how often you pick up your phone.

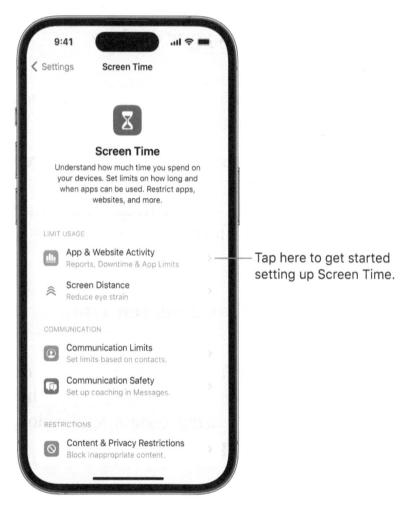

Tap here to get started setting up Screen Time.

Activate Screen Time

Enter the Settings application, touch Screen Time, touch Apps & Websites Activity, and then touch Turn On Apps & Websites Activity.

Use Screen Time on your devices

You can share Screen Time settings with all your devices registered with the same Apple ID.

❖ Enter the Settings application, and touch Screen Time.
❖ Scroll down, and then activate the **Share Across Devices** feature.

See a summary of your Screen Time

After activating Apps & Website Activity, you can view reports about your device usage to check how much time you spend using certain applications, how often you use your phone, etc.

❖ Enter the Settings application, and touch Screen Time.

❖ Touch the **See All Apps & Websites Activity** button, and then touch the **Devices** button to choose one of the devices

❖ Touch the **Day** tab or the **Week** tab to see a summary of your daily or weekly use.

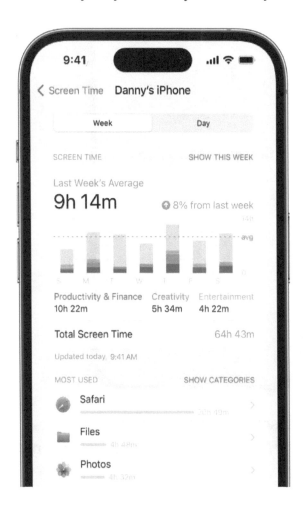

Protect your vision health using the Screen Distance feature

Looking too closely at a device screen (or book) for long periods of time can increase the risk of myopia for young users and eye strain for individuals of all ages. **Screen Distance** makes use of the TrueDepth camera in the front of your device to detect when you hold your phone closer than 12 inches for extended periods of time, and prompts you to move your phone further away.

❖ Enter the Settings application, and touch Screen Time
❖ Touch the **Screen Distance** button, and then activate Screen Distance

When you hold your device very close to your face for a long time, the Screen Distance feature will cover the screen with a warning and prevent you from continuing. When you move your phone more than 30.48cm away, you can touch the **Continue** button to continue using your device.

When your device displays the Screen Distance warning, move your Phone more than 12 inches away, and then touch the **Continue** button when it becomes active.

Schedule time away from your device

You can block notifications & applications for periods when you want time away from your device.

For instance, you can schedule downtime at bedtime.

When Downtime is active, only messages, calls, & applications you choose to allow are available.

❖ Enter the Settings application, and touch Screen Time.
❖ Click on Apps & Websites Activity, and then activate Apps & Websites Activity if you have not already.
❖ Click on the **Downtime** button, and then carry out any of the below:
  ➢ Touch the **Turn on Down-time till Tomorrow** option.
  ➢ Click on the **Schedule** button to schedule downtime.
❖ Choose the Everyday option or the Customize Days option, and then set the beginning and ending times.

You can deactivate the Downtime schedule anytime you want by simply disabling the **Scheduled** option

Set limits on application usage

You can set time limits for app categories (for example, Games or Social Networks) and for individual applications.

❖ Enter the Settings application, and then touch Screen Time
❖ Touch the **Apps Limits** button, and then touch the **Add Limit** button.
❖ Pick one or more application categories.
To set limit for individual applications, click on any of the categories to view all the applications in that category, and then choose the application you'd like to limit. If you select multiple applications or categories, the time limit you set will apply to all of them.
❖ Click on the **Next** button in the upper right part of your display, and then set the time allowed.
Click the **Customize Days** button to set times for each day, and then set limits for specific days.
❖ Touch the **Add** button when you've set the limits.

Choose contacts and applications to allow at all times

You can choose contacts that can call & send messages to you and applications you can use at all times even when Downtime is active.

❖ Enter the Settings application, touch Screen Time, and then touch the **Always Allowed** button

❖ In the **Allowed Apps** section, touch the Add icon⊕ or the Remove icon⊖ beside an application to add or remove the application from the Allowed Applications list.

❖ Click the **Contacts** button to select the contacts you want to allow communications with.
If you pick the **Specific Contacts** option, you can choose any of the options below and then adhere to the directives on your screen:

➢ Add New Contact
➢ Choose From My Contacts

❖ Click on the Back icon〈 in the upper left part of your display.

Check for sensitive images

You can set your phone to detect nudity in pictures before they are sent or received in the Messages application, Face-Time messages, Contact Posters, AirDrop, the Photos application, & 3rd-party applications that support Apple's communication security system. If your device detects nudity in a picture, the picture will be blurred and resources will be provided to help you manage the situation.

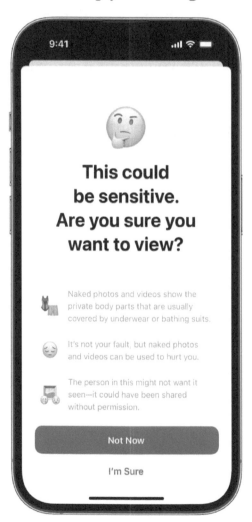

❖ Enter the Settings application, and touch Screen Time.

❖ Click on the **Communication Safety** button, and then activate the Communication Safety feature.

When the **Communication Safety** feature is enabled, your phone will detect nude pictures before they are viewed or sent, and it will display an alert to warn you about the image.

Note: When you activate the Communication Safety feature, it activates Sensitive Content Warning in the Settings application>Privacy and Security.

DOWNLOAD APPS FROM THE APP STORE

You'll find new applications, exclusive stories, tips and tricks, and in-application events in the Apps Store application 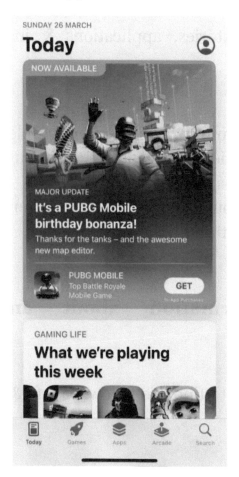.

Note: Your iPhone has to be connected to the internet before you can use the Apps Store.

Find applications

Touch any of the below:

- ❖ Today: Check out stories, applications & in-application events.
- ❖ Apps
- ❖ Games
- ❖ Arcade: Enjoy premium games from Apple Arcade (subscription needed) without advertisements or in-application purchases.
- ❖ Search. Type what you are looking for, and then touch the **Search** button on the keyboard

Get more information about an application

Click on an application to find the following info & more:

- ❖ In-apps event
- ❖ Size of the file

- ❖ Privacy info
- ❖ Family Sharing & Game Centre support
- ❖ Previews or screenshots
- ❖ Support for other Apple devices
- ❖ Reviews & ratings
- ❖ Supported languages

Buy & download an application

- ❖ Click on the **Get** button or the app's price.

  If there's a Redownload icon ⍟ instead of a price or the **Get** button, it means you have already purchased the app, and you can get it for free now. Simply click on the Redownload icon ⍟ to download the app.
- ❖ If necessary, authenticate with Face ID or your passcode to finish the purchase.

Give or share an application

- ❖ Touch the application to view its details.
- ❖ Touch the Share button ⎙, and then choose one of the sharing options or click on the **Gift App** button.

Send or redeem an Apple Gift Card

❖ Click on the Account icon 🔵 or your picture in the upper right corner of your iPhone's display.
❖ Touch any of the below:
  ➢ Send Gift Card via E-mail
  ➢ Redeem Gift Code or Card

Change your Apps Store settings

Enter the Settings application, touch App Store, and then carry out any of the below:

❖ Automatically download applications purchased on your other Apple devices: In the Automatic Downloads section, activate Apps Download.
❖ Update applications automatically: Activate Apps Updates.
❖ Download in-apps content in the background: Activate In-App Contents to download contents before you launch the application for the first time
❖ Allow application downloads to use mobile data: In the Cellular Data section, activate Automatic Downloads. If you want the App Store to ask for permission for downloads above 200MB, simply

touch the **Apps Download** button, and choose the option.

❖ Automatically play application preview videos: Enable the **Video Auto-play** feature

❖ Remove unused applications automatically: Deactivate Offload Unused Apps. You can always reinstall the application if it is still available in the Apps Store.

Set content restrictions and prevent in-application purchases

After activating content and privacy settings, adhere to the directives on your display.

❖ Enter the Settings application, touch Screen Time, touch Content and Privacy Restriction, and then touch Content Restriction.

❖ Set restrictions like the following:
  ➢ Applications: Restrict applications by age rating.
  ➢ Application Clips: Prevent Application Clips from opening.

CAMERA AND PHOTOS APPS

Learn how to take nice pictures with your iPhone's camera.

Open the Camera app

Carry out any of the below to enter the Camera application:

❖ Touch the Camera application's icon  on your Home Screen.

❖ Swipe to the left on the Lock screen.

❖ Swipe down from the upper right corner of your screen to open the Controls Centre, and then click on the Camera button 📷

❖ Press & hold the Camera button  on your Lock screen.

Note: For security reasons, a green dot will always appear in the upper right corner of your screen when your iPhone's Camera is being used

Capture a picture

❖ Launch the Camera application, and then touch the White shutter or press one of the volume buttons to take a picture.

Move from one camera mode to another

The **Photos** mode is the default mode you see anytime you open the Camera application. You can snap Live Photos & still pictures in Photo mode. Swipe right or left on the camera screen to choose any of the camera modes below:

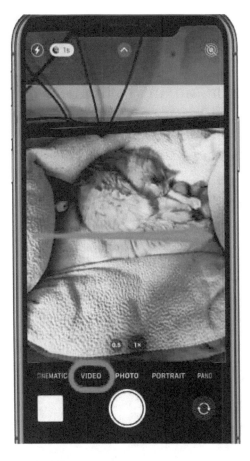

❖ Video

- ❖ Slo-mo: Record a slow motion video
- ❖ Portrait
- ❖ Time-lapse
- ❖ Pano
- ❖ Cinematic
- ❖ Square

Zoom out or in

In the Camera application, do any of the below to zoom out or in:

- ❖ Pinch open on the Camera screen to zoom in or pinch closed to zoom out.
- ❖ Switch between 0.50x, 1.0x, 2x, 2.50x, 3x & 5.0x to zoom out or in. To get a more precise zoom, press & hold the zoom controls, and then slide the slider to the left or right.

Change the camera's exposure & focus

Before capturing a picture, your iPhone's camera automatically determines the exposure & focus, and face detection balances the exposure of many faces. Follow the directives below to manually change the exposure & focus:

❖ Enter the Camera app.
❖ Touch your camera screen to see the automatic exposure setting & focus area
❖ Touch where you want the focus to be

❖ Drag the Adjust Exposure icon ☀ close to the focus area down or up to change the exposure level.

Tip: To manually lock your exposure & focus settings for future shots, press & hold the focus area till the AE/AF lock appears on your display; touch your screen to unlock the settings.

To save the exposure control so it isn't reset when you close & reopen the Camera app, simply head over to the Settings app, tap Camera, tap Preserve Setting, and then enable Exposure Adjustment.

Camera flashlight

The camera will automatically use the flashlight when required. Before snapping a picture, do the following for manual control of the flashlight:

❖ Touch the Flashlight icon ⚡ to turn the flashlight on or off.

❖ Click on the Camera Controls icon⌃, and then click on the Flash icon⚡ under the frame to select Off, On, or Auto.

Snap a picture with a filter

Use filters to add colour effects to your pictures.

❖ Enter the Camera app, and then select Portrait or Photos mode.
❖ Tap on the Camera Control icon⌃, and then touch the Filters icon⊕.
❖ Swipe right or left to see filters under the viewer; touch any of them to use it.
❖ Touch the White Shutter to capture a picture with the filter you selected.

Use the timer

Set a timer to give yourself time to get in the shot.

❖ Launch the Camera app, touch the Camera Controls icon⌃

❖ Tap the Timers icon⟳, and then select 10 seconds or 3 seconds
❖ Touch the Shutter to begin the timer.

Use Photographic Styles

Photographic Styles customize how your iPhone camera snaps pictures. Select from the preset styles—Cool, Warm, Vibrant, or Rich Contrast— and then change the warmth & tones value to personalize them. The Camera app will apply your settings every time it takes a picture in Photos mode. Follow the directives below to use another Photographic Style:

❖ Enter the Camera app, and then touch the Camera Controls icon⌃.

❖ Touch the Photos Style icon, and then swipe to the left to check out different styles:
  ➢ Cool.
  ➢ Warm.
  ➢ Vibrant.
  ➢ Rich Contrast.

To personalize a Photo Style, touch the Warmth & Tone controls under the frame, and then slide the slider to the right or left to change the value. Touch the Reset button◯ to reset the values.

❖ Touch the Photo Styles icon to use the Photos Style.

To change or edit your preset Photos Style, click on the Photos Style icon  in the upper part of your iPhone's display. To stop making use of a Photo Style, choose **Standard** from the Photo style options.

You can also change the Photos Style in the Setting app: head over to the Settings app, click on Camera, click on Photographic Styles, and then choose one of them.

Capture Live Photos

A Live Photo captures what takes place just before & after you capture a picture.

❖ Launch the Camera app.
❖ Ensure the Camera is in Photos mode & that Live Photo is enabled.
  When Live Photo is active, you will see the Live Photo icon ◎ in the upper part of your iPhone camera display. When there's a slash through the Live Photos icon it means that the Live Photo is off. Touch the button to activate or disable Live Photo.
❖ Touch the White Shutter to capture the Live Photo.
❖ To play the Live Photo, touch the thumbnail in the lower part of your screen, and then long-press your screen to play it.

Take action photos with Burst mode

Burst mode allows your iPhone to capture moving subjects, or capture many high-speed images so that you have a range of pictures to pick from. You can use the front & back cameras to capture burst images.

❖ Head over to the Camera app.
❖ Swipe the Shutter to the left

❖ Raise your finger to stop taking pictures

❖ To choose the pictures you'd like to keep, touch the Burst thumbnail, and then click on the **Select** button.
The gray dots under the thumbnails indicate the recommended images to keep on your phone.

❖ Touch the circle in the bottom-right edge of any photo you want to store as a separate picture, and then click on the **Done** button.

To delete the whole set of Burst pictures, simply touch the thumbnail, and then click on the Delete icon 🗑

Tip: You can also long-press the Increase Volume button on your iPhone to snap Burst photos. Head over to the Settings app, tap on Camera, and then enable the **Use Volume Up for Burst** feature.

Snap a photo or record a video with your iPhone's front-facing camera

❖ Launch the Camera app.

❖ Click on the Camera Selector icon ⊚ to switch to the front camera.

❖ Select Video, Photos, Portrait, etc.

❖ Place your phone in front of you.

Tip: Touch the arrow inside the frame to increase the view area.

❖ Touch the Shutter or press one of your iPhone's volume buttons to snap a picture or record a video.

To snap a selfie that takes the shot as you see it on the front camera, instead of reversing it, head over to the Settings app, click on Camera, and then activate the **Mirror Front Camera** feature.

Capture panoramic pictures

Use your iPhone's camera to snap panoramic pictures of your surroundings.

❖ Launch the Camera app.
❖ Swipe the mode selector to Pano mode.
❖ Touch the White Shutter
❖ Move slowly in the arrow's direction, while making sure it's on the middle line.
❖ To finish, click the Shutter one more time.

Touch the arrow to pan in the other direction. Turn your phone to landscape orientation to pan vertically.

Capture macro videos & photos

You can use your camera to capture amazingly clear
close-up pictures & videos.

Capture macro videos or pictures

- ❖ Launch the Camera app, and then swipe the Camera mode selector to Video or Photos mode
- ❖ Move close to the subject—as close as 2cm. Your iPhone's camera will automatically use the Ultra-Wide lens.

- ❖ Touch the Shutter to snap a picture or the Record button to start & stop recording a video.

Capture a macro slow-motion video

- ❖ Launch the Camera app, and then swipe the camera mode selector to Slo-mo mode
- ❖ Touch 0.50x to use the Ultra Wide lens, and then go near the subject.
- ❖ Click on the Record button to record & stop recording the video.

Control automatic macro switching

You can control when your iPhone's camera automatically uses the Ultra-Wide lens to capture macro pictures & videos.

❖ Launch the Camera app, and then go near your subject
When you enter the macro range of your subject, the Macro icon 🌺 will appear on your display.

❖ Click on the Macro icon 🌺 to disable automatic macro switching.

❖ Click on the Macro button⬤ one more time to re-activate automatic macro switching.

To disable automatic switching to the Ultra-Wide lens for macro videos & pictures, simply enter the Settings app, tap Camera, and then deactivate Macro Control.

If you would like to keep your Macro Control settings between camera sessions, simply enter the Settings application, tap Camera, touch Preserve Settings, and then activate Macro Control.

Snap photos in Portrait mode

Portrait mode uses depth-of-field effects to keep the subject of your picture sharp while creating a blurred background.

Take a photo in portrait mode

❖ Launch the Camera app and then swipe the camera mode selector to Portrait mode.
❖ If prompted, follow the instructions on your display to put your subject in the yellow box.

Tap 1.0x, 2.0x, or 3.0x to switch from one zoom option to another.

Or, pinch open on your display to zoom in and pinch closed to zoom out.

❖ Drag the Portrait Lighting control to use one of the lighting effects:

- ➢ High-Key Light Mono
- ➢ Stage Light Mono
- ➢ Stage Light
- ➢ Contour Light.
- ➢ Studio Light.
- ➢ Natural light.
- ❖ Touch the White Shutter on your screen to snap the picture.

After snapping a picture in Portrait mode, you can remove the portrait mode effect at any time. To do this, simply open the picture in the Photos application on your iPhone, touch the **Edit** button, and then touch the **Portrait** button to activate or disable the effect.

Adjust Depth Control in Portrait mode

Use the Depth control slider to adjust the amount of background blur in your image.

- ❖ Enter the Camera application, swipe the camera selector to Portrait mode, and then frame your subject.
- ❖ Click the Adjust Depth icon 𝑓 in the upper right corner of your display.
  Next, you'll see the Depth Control Slider under the frame.

❖ Drag the slider to the left or right to change the effect level

❖ Touch the Shutter button to snap the picture.

After taking a portrait, you can use the Depth Controls slider in the Photos application to further change the background blur effects.

Adjust the Portrait Lighting in Portrait mode

You can change the intensity & position of the Portrait Lighting in photos to brighten facial features.

❖ Enter the Camera application, swipe the Camera mode selector to Portrait mode, and then drag the Portrait Lighting control 🔷 to choose one of the lighting effects.

❖ Click the Portrait Management button 🔘 in the upper part of your display.
Next, you'll see the Portrait Lighting slider under the frame.

❖ Move the slider to the left or right to change the effect level.

❖ Touch the Shutter button to snap the picture.

Capture a portrait in Photos mode

You can apply the portrait effect in images captured in the Photos mode.

❖ Launch the Camera app.
If your device detects an individual, cat, or dog, the Depth icon 𝒇 will automatically appear under the view finder.
Note: Your phone captures depth info when the Depth icon 𝒇 appears while capturing pictures in Photos mode, so if you choose not to use the portrait effects when you snap the picture, you can use it later in the Photos application.

Tap to turn portrait effects on and off in Photo mode.

❖ If the Depth icon 🄵 does not appear, touch a subject to make it the point of focus, and the Depth icon 🄵 will appear. Touch another subject on your screen to make it the new point of focus.

❖ Click on the Depth icon 🄵, and then touch the White Shutter to capture the picture with the portrait effects.

Capture Night-mode pictures

Night Mode allows your camera to snap more detail & brighten your photos in low-light conditions.

❖ Launch the Camera app. Night mode activates automatically in low-light situations.

❖ Click on the Night Mode icon ⊜ at the upper part of your camera display to activate or disable Night Mode.

❖ To experiment with Night Mode, touch the Camera Control button ⌃, touch the Night Mode icon ⊜ in the options bar at the lower part of your camera screen, and move the slider to the right or left to select between Max & Auto timers. Max makes use of the longest exposure time; "Auto" sets the time automatically. Your selected settings are saved for the next night mode shot.

- Click on the White Shutter, and then set your phone to take the picture (ensure your device is still)
Crosshairs will appear on your camera screen if your device detects motion while you're taking the picture—simply align the crosshairs to reduce motion & make the shot better.
To stop capturing a Night Mode picture mid-capture, simply touch **Stop** under the slider.

Change the shutter sound volume

- Launch the Camera app, and select Photos mode.
- Swipe down from the upper right corner of your screen to open the Controls Centre, and then drag the volume slider 🔊 down or up
- Swipe up to return to the Camera application

Capture Apple ProRAW pictures

Apple ProRAW combines standard RAW format data with iPhone image processing to provide more creative control when you adjust white balance, colour & exposure.

Setup Apple ProRAW

Navigate to the Settings app, click on Camera, click Formats, and then enable ProRAW & Resolution Control.

Capture images with Apple ProRAW

❖ In the Camera app, touch the ProRAW icon (RAW) or RAW MAX to activate ProRAW.

❖ Snap pictures
   While shooting, you can toggle between the Raw On (RAW) or RAW MAX and Raw Off RAW MAX buttons to activate or disable the ProRAW feature
   To save your ProRAW settings, launch the Settings app, tap Camera, tap Preserve Settings, and then enable ProRAW & Resolution Control.

Change the default resolution and format of Apple ProRAW

You can set the ProRAW default resolution to 12MP, 48MP, or HEIF 48MP.

❖ Launch the Settings app, tap Camera, and then tap Formats.

- ❖ Activate ProRAW & Resolution Controls
- ❖ Click on Pro Default, and then select ProRAW Max, Pro RAW 12MP, or HEIF Max as your default format & resolution.

Record videos

- ❖ Enter the Camera app, and then swipe the mode selector to Video mode.
- ❖ Touch the Record button or press any of the volume buttons to record the video. While recording, you can:
  - ➢ Click on the White Shutter to snap a picture.
  - ➢ Pinch open on your camera display to zoom in & pinch closed to zoom out.
  - ➢ Long-press 1x, and then drag the slider to zoom out or zoom in
- ❖ Click on the Record button to stop recording the video.

Note: For safety reasons, a green dot will always appear in the upper part of your display when your iPhone's camera is being used.

Record 4k or HD videos

You can use your phone to record videos in high-definition formats such as 4K (PAL), HD (PAL), HD, & 4K.

❖ Enter the Settings app, click on Camera, and then click on the **Record Video** button.
❖ Select video formats & frame rates from the list.

Use Action Mode

Action mode provides better stability when you record in Video mode. Click on the Action Mode On icon ⊗ in the upper part of your camera display to activate Action Mode & touch the Action Mode Off icon 🏃 to disable it.

Note: Action mode functions better in bright light. If you want to use Action mode in low-light, enter the Settings application, touch Camera, touch Record Video, and then enable Action Mode Lower Light. The maximum capture resolution of the Action mode is 2.80K.

Record ProRes videos

You can record & edit videos in ProRes, which provides less compression & better colour fidelity.

Setup ProRes

To configure ProRes, navigate to the Settings app, click on Camera, click Formats, and then enable Apple ProRes.

Record a ProRes video

❖ In the Camera app, swipe to Video mode, and then touch the ProRes icon ^{ProRes}_{HDR} to enable ProRes.
❖ Touch the Record button to start and stop recording the video.
❖ Click on the ProRes button ^{ProRes}_{HDR} to disable ProRes

Select the colour encoding option for your ProRes recordings

You can choose Log, SDR, HDR, colour encoding when recording videos in ProRes.

❖ Enter the Settings app, click on Camera, touch Formats, and then enable Apple ProRes.
❖ Click on ProRes Encoding, and then choose one of the options.

Record Quick-Take videos

A Quick-Take video is a video recorded in Photos mode. While recording a QuickTake video, you can put the Record button in the lock position & take still pictures.

Page | 293

❖ Enter the Camera app, ensure the camera is in Photos mode, and then long-press the Shutter to record a Quick-Take video.

❖ Slide the shutter button to the right & raise your finger when it is in Lock position for hands-free recording.

➢ Swipe up to zoom in on what you're recording, or if you are recording hands-free, pinch open on your camera display to zoom in

➢ You will see the Shutter & Record button under the frame—touch the White Shutter to capture photos while recording

❖ Click on the Record button to stop recording the video.

Tip: Long-press one of the volume buttons to record a Quick-Take video in Photos mode.

Touch the thumb-nail to check out the QuickTake video in the Photos application.

Record a slow motion video

When recording in Slo-mo mode, the video is recorded at normal speed and you can only see the slow motion effect when you play the video. You can also choose when the Slow motion effect starts & stops in the video.

❖ Launch the Camera app, and then swipe the camera mode selector to Slo-mo mode.

You can tap the Switch Camera icon🔄 to use the front-facing camera

❖ Touch the Record button to record the video. While recording, you can click on the White Shutter to take a picture.

❖ Click on the Record button to stop recording the video.

To slow down part of the video and play the rest at normal speed, touch the video thumb-nail and then touch the **Edit** button. Drag the vertical bar under the frame viewer to specify the part you want to play in slow motion.

To change slow-motion recording settings, simply enter the Settings application, touch Camera, and then touch Record Slo-mo.

Record videos in Cinematic mode

The Cinematic mode makes use of depth-of-field effects that keep the subject of a video sharp while creating a blurred background. Your phone automatically detects the subject of the video and keeps it in focus during recording; your iPhone will automatically move the focus point when it identifies a new subject. You can also manually change the focus point while recording or edit it later in the Photo application.

❖ Launch the Camera app, and swipe the Camera mode selector to Cinematic mode.
   ➢ To adjust the depth effects, touch the Adjust Depth icon 𝑓 and then drag the slider to the right or left before you start recording.
❖ Touch the Record button to record the video.
   ➢ The yellow frame on your camera display indicates the subject in focus; a gray box

indicates a newly identified individual, but not in focus. Touch the gray frame to change the point of focus; touch the box once more to lock the point of focus on the individual.

➢ If there is nobody in the video, touch anywhere on your iPhone's display to set the point of focus.

➢ Long-press your screen to lock the point of focus at a distance.

❖ Click on the Record button to stop recording the video.

Activate or deactivate Enhanced Stabilization

The Enhanced Stabilization feature zooms in a little to provide better stabilization when you record in Video mode & Cinematic mode. This feature is enabled by default.

To deactivate this feature, simply enter the Settings application, touch Camera, touch Record Video, and then deactivate Enhanced Stabilization.

Adjust the main camera lens

The default for the 1x Main lens on your phone is 24mm. You can add 28mm & 35mm as additional lenses, and choose a new default Main lens.

❖ Head over to the Settings app, tap Camera, tap Formats, tap Photos Mode, and then click 24MP.
❖ Enter the Setting app, click Camera, and then click on Main Camera.

❖ In the Additional Lenses segment, activate the lenses you'd like to add as secondary Main lenses.

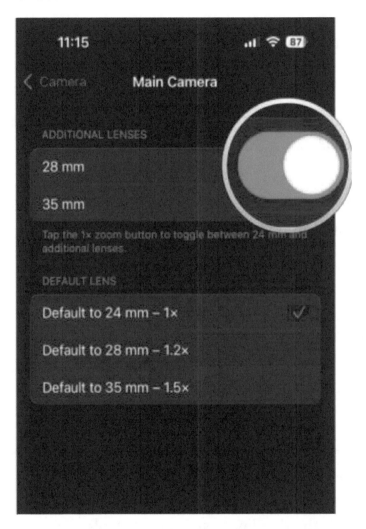

❖ Under Default Lens, click on any of the options to use it as the default Main lens.

❖ Exit the Settings application.

After setting up the Main camera lens, enter the Camera app. The Main camera's default lens will be the one you picked in the Settings application. Tap the Main camera lens to move to one of the additional lenses.

Change the resolution of the Main Camera

The default resolution of the Main camera is 24MP. You can switch between 48MP, 24MP, & 12MP.

Launch the Settings app, click on Camera, click on Format, tap Photos Mode, and then pick one of the options.

View your pictures

❖ Touch the thumbnail in the lower left edge of your display in the Camera app.
❖ Swipe to view your latest pictures.
❖ Touch the display to see the controls
❖ Click on the **All Photos** button to view all the videos & pictures stored in the Photos app.

Share your pictures

Click on the Share button⬆ in an image and then choose one of the sharing options.

Use your iPhone's camera to scan QR codes

You can use your iPhone's camera to scan QR codes for tickets, sites, coupons, etc.

❖ Launch the Camera app, and then set your phone in a way that the code can be seen clearly on your camera screen.
❖ Click on the notification that pops-up on your display to enter the appropriate site or application.

Open the Code Scanner from the Controls Centre

❖ Enter the Settings application, touch Controls Centre, and then touch the Add icon⊕ beside Code Scanner

Page | 303

❖ Swipe down from the upper right corner of your display, touch the **Code Scanner** button, and then set your phone in a way that the code can be seen clearly on your screen.
❖ Activate the flashlight to add more light.

Use Live Text with your camera

Your iPhone's camera can translate, share, & copy texts that appear on the camera screen. The camera allows you to easily dial phone numbers, access sites, convert money, etc., based on the text that appears in the frame.

❖ Launch the Camera app, and then set your phone in a way that the text can be seen clearly on your display.
❖ When you see a yellow box around the visible text, simply touch the Live Text icon and then carry out any of the below:

- ➢ Click on the **Copy** button to copy the text.
- ➢ Tap the **Select All** button to highlight all the text.
- ➢ Tap the **Lookup** button to see web recommendations.
- ➢ Tap on the **Translate** button to translate the text
- ➢ Click on the **Share** button to share the text with any of the sharing options.

Or, long-press the text, then select the text you want with the grab points, and then perform any of the actions above.

Click on any of the quick actions in the lower part of your iPhone display to do things like go to a webpage, begin an e-mail, make a call, etc.

❖ Touch the Live Text button 🔲 to go back to the Camera.

To disable the **Live Text** feature on your iPhone's camera, head over to the Setting app, click on Camera, and then disable the **Live Text** feature.

View videos & pictures in the Photos app

You will find all the videos & pictures on your phone in the Photos app.

How videos & pictures are arranged on your device

You can surf through the Photos app using the Search, Albums, For You, & Library tabs in the lower part of your display.

Tap to navigate Photos.

View pictures in your library

To see your pictures & videos by when you snapped or recorded them, click on the **Library** tab, and then choose any of the below:

* ❖ Days
* ❖ Months
* ❖ Years
* ❖ All Photos: See all your videos & pictures

View pictures in full-screen

Tap one of the pictures to display it in full screen on your phone.

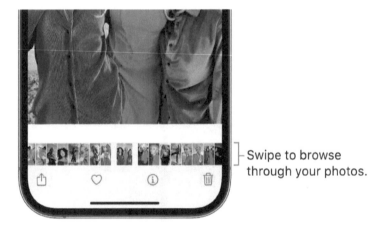

Swipe to browse through your photos.

Pinch open on your display to zoom in on the picture and pinch closed to zoom out.

You can also double-tap the picture to zoom in or out.

Touch the Favorite icon ♡ to add the picture to your Favourites album.

Tip: When viewing a Live Photo ◎, long-press the picture to play it.

Click on the Back icon ‹ to continue browsing.

Click on the Trash icon 🗑 to delete the picture

View video & picture info

Tap a circle to name someone identified in the photo.

To view the metadata info stored in a video or picture, open the video or picture, and then touch the Info button ⓘ.

Play a video

While browsing videos and pictures in the Photos application, touch one of the videos you've recorded or stored on your phone to play it. While the video plays, you can:

❖ Touch the controls under the video to delete, share, favourite, unmute/mute, pause, or display the video info; touch the display to hide the controls.

❖ Double-tap your display to switch between fit-to-display & full screen.

❖ Long-press the frame viewer in the lower part of your display to pause the video, then slide the viewer to the right or left to move forward or back.

Make & play slideshows

Create a slideshow to watch a collection of videos & pictures that you select from your library. Slideshows are automatically organized and set to music.

❖ Click on the **Library** button, and then view your pictures by Days or All Photos.

❖ Click on the **Select** button.

❖ Touch the pictures you want to add to the slideshow, and then touch the More Options icon⊙.

❖ Touch the **Slideshow** button from the options list.

To change the slideshow's music, theme, and more, simply touch your screen while the slideshow is playing, and then touch **Options**.

Note: You can also create a slideshow from one of your albums. Click Albums, touch the album you'd like to create the slideshow from, and then adhere to the directives above.

Delete videos & pictures

In the Photos application, you can delete videos & pictures from your phone.

❖ Delete a video or picture: To delete a video or picture from your phone, touch the video or picture, and then touch the Delete icon 🗑.

Deleted videos & pictures are stored in the Recently Deleted album for thirty days, where you can restore them or permanently erase them from your device.

❖ Delete multiple videos & pictures: While viewing pictures in an album or the All Photos or Days view in your library, touch the **Select** button, touch the items you want to delete, and then touch the Delete icon 🗑.

Recover or permanently erase deleted pictures & videos

❖ Enter the Photos application, touch Albums, swipe up, and then touch **Recently Deleted** in the Utilities section

❖ Touch the **Select** button, and then touch the videos and pictures you'd like to delete or recover

❖ Touch the More Options icon⊙ in the lower part of your display, and then touch the **Delete** button or the **Recover** button

Hide videos & pictures

Adhere to the directives below to hide pictures and videos in the Photos application:

❖ Hide a video or picture: Touch the video or picture, touch the Hide icon⊙, and then touch the **Hide** button in the options list.

Hidden pictures are sent to the Hidden album. To deactivate Hidden Album so it does not appear in Albums, enter the Settings application, touch Photos, and then disable Hidden Album

❖ Hide multiple videos & pictures: While viewing pictures in an album or the All Photos or Days view in your library, touch the **Select** button, touch the items you want to hide, touch the More Options icon ⊙, and then touch the **Hide** button.

Unlock the Recently Deleted & Hidden albums

Recently Deleted and Hidden albums are locked by default. Simply use your Face ID or passcode to unlock these albums.

To change the settings from locked to unlocked, enter the Settings application, touch Photos, and then deactivate Use Passcode.

Edit videos and pictures

After taking a picture or recording a video, use tools in the Photos application to edit it.

Adjust colour & light

❖ In the Photos application, touch a video or picture thumbnail to show it in full screen.

❖ Click on the **Edit** button, and then swipe under the picture to check out the effects you can edit such as Shadows, Exposure, etc.

❖ Touch the effect you would like to edit, and then drag the slider to adjust the effect.
After making the adjustments, touch the effect button to toggle between the modified effect and the original.

❖ Click on the **Done** button to save your changes, or touch the **Cancel** button if you do not like the changes you've made, and then touch the **Discard Changes** button.

Tip: Click on the Enhance button to automatically use effects to edit your videos or pictures.

Crop, flip, or rotate photos or videos

❖ In the Photos application, touch one of the video or picture thumbnails to show it in full screen.

❖ Click on the **Edit** button, click on the Crop icon , and then carry out any of the below:

➢ Crop manually: Drag the corners to outline the area you would like to keep in the picture.

➢ Crop to a custom fixed aspect ratio: Click the Freeform Aspect Ratio icon , then choose one of the options like 5:4, wallpaper, square, etc.

➢ Rotate: Click on the Rotate icon to rotate the image 90 degrees.

➢ Flip: Click the Flip icon to flip the picture.

Tap to undo a crop.

❖ Click on the **Done** button to save the changes you've made, or touch the **Cancel** button if you do not like the adjustments, and then click on the **Discard Changes** button.

To quickly crop a picture while viewing it, zoom in on the picture, drag the photo around to show the part you want, and then touch the **Crop** button in the upper right part of your display. Make additional adjustments using the crop tools, and then touch the **Done** button.

Adjust & straighten perspective

❖ In the Photos application, touch one of the video or picture thumbnails to show it in full screen.
❖ Click on the **Edit** button, and then touch the Crop icon ⌗.
❖ Swipe left below the picture to see the editable effects: Horizontal, Vertical, Straight.
❖ Touch the effect you would like to edit, and then drag the slider to adjust the effect.
After making the adjustments, touch the effect button to toggle between the modified effect and the original.
❖ Click on the **Done** button to save your changes, or touch the **Cancel** button if you do not like the

changes you've made, and then touch the **Discard Changes** button.

Apply the filter effects

- ❖ In the Photos application, touch one of the video or picture thumbnails to show it in full screen.
- ❖ Click on the **Edit** button, and then touch the Filters icon⊛ to use filter effects like Dramatic, or Mono.
- ❖ Touch one of the filters, and then slide the slider to make adjustments to the effect
Touch the picture to compare the edited picture to the original
- ❖ Click on the **Done** button to save your changes, or touch the **Cancel** button if you do not like the changes you've made, and then touch the **Discard Changes** button.

Undo & redo edits

When editing a video or picture, touch the Undo icon⟲ and the Redo icon⟳ in the upper part of your display to undo and redo multiple editing steps.

Tip: Touch the video or picture to toggle between the edited version and the original.

Copy and paste edits to multiple images

You can copy your edits from one picture and paste them onto another picture or a set of pictures at the same time.

❖ Open the picture that has the edits you'd like to copy

❖ Touch the More Options icon ⊙ , and then touch the **Copy Edits** button

❖ Touch the Back icon ‹ to go back to your photos library

❖ Touch the **Select** button, and then touch the picture(s) you want to paste the edits onto

❖ Touch the More Options icon ⊙ , and then touch the **Paste Edits** button.

Revert an edited video or picture

After editing a video or picture and saving the changes you've made, you can revert to the original.

❖ Open the edited video or picture, and then touch the More Options icon ⊙ .

❖ Touch the **Revert to Original** button.

Change the location, time, or date

You can change the location, time, & date stored in the video or photo's metadata info.

- ❖ Open the video or picture, and then touch the More Options icon ⊙.
- ❖ Click on Adjust Location or Adjust Time & Date.

To change the location, time, or date of a group of pictures, touch the **Select** button, touch the pictures, and then adhere to the directives above.

You can revert a video or picture to its original location, time, or date. Touch the More Options icon ⊙, touch Adjust Location or Adjust Time & Date, and then touch the **Revert** button.

Draw or write on a picture

- ❖ In the Photos application, touch a picture to show it in full screen.
- ❖ Touch the **Edit** button, and then touch the Markup icon Ⓐ.
- ❖ Use the different colours & tools to write or draw on the picture. Click the Add Annotation button ＋ to magnify or add shapes, text, captions, etc.
- ❖ When you are done, touch the **Done** button to save your changes

Or, touch the **Cancel** button if you do not like the changes.

Cut a video

You can trim a video to change where it starts & stops.

❖ In the Photos application, open the video, and then click the **Edit** button.
❖ To change the start and stop times, drag the end of the frame viewer under the video, and then touch the **Done** button.
❖ Click the **Save Video** button to keep only the cut video, or touch the **Save Video as a New Clip** button to keep both versions of the video.

To undo the trim after saving the video, simply open the video, touch the **Edit** button, and then touch the **Revert** button.

Note: Videos saved as new clips cannot be reverted to the original.

Change the slow motion part of a video captured in Slo-mo mode

You can change the part of a video that appears in slow motion when you record in slo-mo mode.

❖ Open the video, and then touch the **Edit** button.
❖ Drag the vertical bar under the frame viewer to specify the part you want to play in slow motion.

Use albums in the Photos application

Use albums to view and organize your videos and pictures. Click on the **Albums** tab to see your videos & pictures arranged into different media types & categories, such as Slo-mo, videos, etc.

Tap to create a new album or folder.

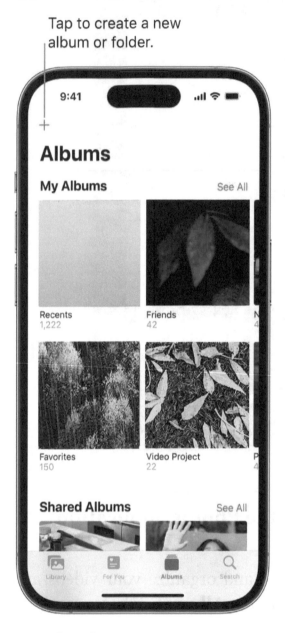

Create an album

❖ Touch the **Albums** tab in the lower part of your display.

❖ Touch the Add icon✝, and then touch the **New Album** button.

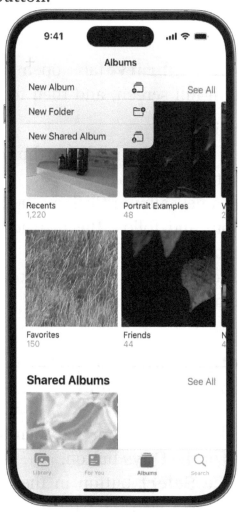

❖ Give the album a name, and then touch the **Save** button.
❖ Touch the videos & pictures you want to add to the album, and then touch the **Add** icon.

Add a video or picture from your library to an album

❖ Touch the **Library** tab, open the video or picture in full screen, and then touch the More Options icon ⊙ .
❖ Click on the **Add to Album** button, and then carry out any of the below:
  ➢ Start a new album: Click on the **New Album** button, and follow the instructions on your screen.
  ➢ Add to one of your albums: Touch one of the albums under My Albums.

Add multiple videos & pictures from your photos library to an album

❖ Touch the **Library** tab, and then touch the **All Photos** or the **Days** button.
❖ Touch the **Select** button in the upper part of your display, touch the videos and pictures you

want to add, and then touch the More Options icon ⓧ .

❖ Click on the **Add to Album** button, and then carry out any of the below:

➢ Start a new album: Click on the **New Album** button, and follow the directives on your screen.

➢ Add to one of your albums: Touch one of the albums under My Albums.

Change the name of an album

You can change the name of the albums you created in the Photos application.

❖ Touch the **Albums** tab, and then touch the album you want to change its name.

❖ Click on the More Options icon ⁝⁝⁝ , and then touch the **Rename Album** button

❖ Type the name of the album in the text area, and then touch the **Save** button.

Watch memories in the Photos application

The Memories feature creates curated collections of videos & pictures that are set to music and you can watch it like a movie. You can also create your own memories and share them with others.

Play a memory

❖ Enter the Photos application, and touch the **For You** tab.
❖ Swipe left under Memories, or touch the **See All** button to check out your memories.
❖ Touch one of the memories to play it. While watching the memory, you can:
  ➢ Pause: Long-press your display, or touch the screen, and then touch the Pause icon ❚❚ in the lower part of your display.
  ➢ Go forward or back: Swipe right or left on your display. You can also touch the display, and then slide the frames in the lower part of your display right or left.
  ➢ Close a memory: Touch your display, and then touch the Cancel icon ✕

Create memories

You can create memories from an event, an album, or a day.

❖ Touch the **Library** tab, touch the **Months** or **Days** button, and then touch the More Options icon ⬤. Or, touch the **Albums** button, open one of your albums, and then touch the More Options icon ⦙⦙⦙ .

❖ Touch the **Play Memory Video** button.

Sharing memories

❖ Touch the **For You** button, and then play the memory you'd like to share
❖ As the memory plays, touch your display, touch the Share icon ⬆, and then select one of the sharing options.

Add memories to Favourites

Touch the **For You** button, and then touch the Favourite icon ♡ in the upper right edge of the memory. Or while the memory is playing, touch your display, touch the More Options icon ⊙, and then touch the **Add To Favourites** button.

To see all your Favourite memories, touch the **For You** button, touch **See All** beside Memories, and then touch **Favourites**.

Delete a memory

❖ Touch the **For You** button, and then touch the More Options icon⊙ in the upper right corner of the memory.
❖ Click on the **Delete Memory** button.

Add a Memory mix

Memory mix is a combination of different songs, styles, & pacing that changes the feel & look of a memory.

❖ Touch the **For You** button, and then touch one of the memories to play it.
❖ Touch your display, and then touch the Memory Mixes icon♫.

❖ Swipe left to see the available Memory mixes.
❖ Touch your display to use a Memory mix

Change the Memory look

❖ Play a memory, and then touch your display.
❖ Touch the Memory Mix icon 🎵, and then touch the Filters icon ⊛
❖ Touch one of the Memory looks, and then touch the **Done** button.

Change the music

❖ Play a memory, and then touch your display.
❖ Touch the Memory Mix icon 🎵, and then touch the Music icon 🎵
Apple Music subscribers can click the Search icon 🔍 to search for songs in their Music library.
❖ Touch one of the songs, and then touch the **Done** button.

Add or remove pictures

- ❖ Play a memory, and then touch your display.
- ❖ Touch the More Options icon⊙, touch the **Manage Photos** button, and then carry out any of the below:
  - ➤ Add featured photos: Touch the pictures in the photo grid that do not have checkmarks to add them to the memory.
    To remove a picture, simply unselect it.
  - ➤ Add photos from your photo library: Tap **All**, scroll, and then touch the pictures you'd like to add.
- ❖ Touch the **Done** button

Rearrange pictures in a memory

- ❖ Play a memory, touch your screen, then touch the Browse icon ▦
- ❖ Touch one of the photos, and then drag it to another position in the grid
- ❖ Touch the Back icon ❮ to go back to the memory.

Export videos & pictures to an external storage device

You can export videos & pictures you captured on your phone directly to a memory card, external drive, or other storage devices.

Note: For edited videos & pictures, the unedited original version will be exported.

❖ Use the Lightning or USB-C connector to connect your phone to the storage device, or connect the device directly to your phone.
❖ Launch the Photos application, and then select the videos & pictures you would like to export
❖ Touch the Share icon⬆️, and then touch the **Export Unmodified Original** button
❖ Touch your storage device in the Locations section, and then touch the **Save** button

FACETIME

Use the Face-Time application to connect face-to-face with loved ones—over WiFi or mobile connection.

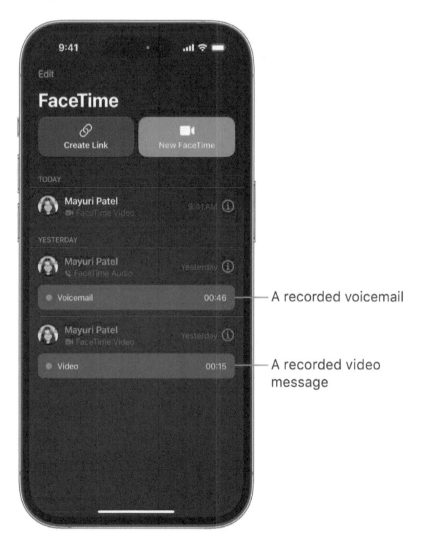

A recorded voicemail

A recorded video message

Setup FaceTime

To setup FaceTime, enter the Settings application, touch FaceTime, and then enable **FaceTime**. Under "You can be reached by Face-Time at," insert your number or Apple ID, if you have not.

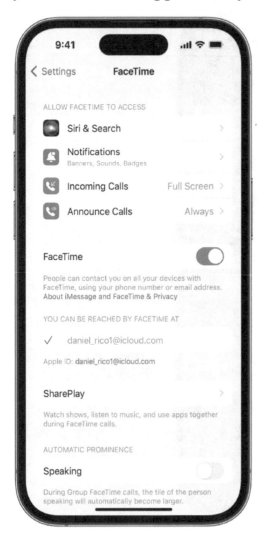

Make a FaceTime call

With connection to the internet (via WiFi or cellular network) and an Apple ID, you can make and receive Face-Time calls.

❖ Launch the FaceTime application, and then touch the **New FaceTime** button.
❖ Type the phone number or name of the person you want to call in the input field, then touch the FaceTime Video icon to make a video call or touch the Voice Call icon to make a voice call.

You can also touch the Add Contact button ⊕ to launch the Contacts application and add someone from there; or touch one of the suggested contacts in your calls history.

Record a video message

If the person you are calling does not answer your Face-Time video call, you can record a video message in the FaceTime application and send it to the person.

❖ Click on the **Record Video** button, and then record your message after the 5-second countdown.

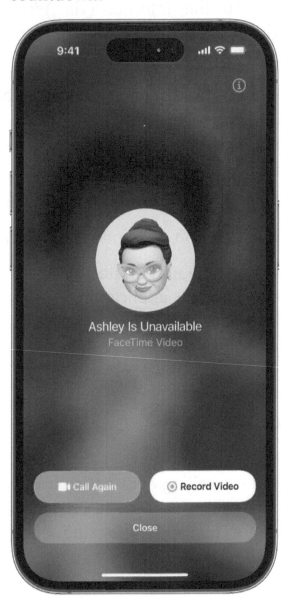

❖ Touch the Send icon ↑ to send the message you recorded, or click on the **Retake** button to record the message again. You can also click on the **Save** button to save the message in the Photos application.

After sending the message, the recipient will receive a notification.

Note: You can only receive video messages from contacts you have saved, individuals you have called, and individuals suggested by Siri.

Leave a voicemail

If somebody does not answer your Face-Time voice call and the individual you are calling has Live Voicemail activated in the Settings application> Phone, you'll be prompted to leave a voicemail.

If you leave a voicemail, your message is written on their screen as you speak, letting them know why you are calling and giving them the opportunity to answer your call.

Answer FaceTime calls

When somebody calls you via FaceTime, carry out any of the below:

❖ Accept a call: Touch the **Accept** button.

❖ Reject a call: Touch the Cancel icon ⊗ or touch the **Decline** button.

❖ Touch the **Message** button to send a text message to the person calling.

❖ Touch the **Remind Me** button to set a reminder to call the person back later.

If you are on a call when a Face-Time video call comes in, instead of the **Accept** button, you'll see the **End & Accept** button, which ends the current call and connects you to the next one.

Listen to Live Voicemails or video messages

If you missed a video call & the caller leaves a video message, you'll be sent a notification that you can touch to watch the message. You can only receive video messages from contacts you have saved, individuals you have called, and individuals suggested by Siri.

If you miss an incoming voice call and you have Voicemail activated in the Settings application>Phone, the caller will be prompted to leave a voicemail. You'll see a real-time transcription of the voicemails and you can answer the call as they are leaving the message.

After the caller sends the video message or voicemail, a link to the message will appear in your Face-Time call history under their call.

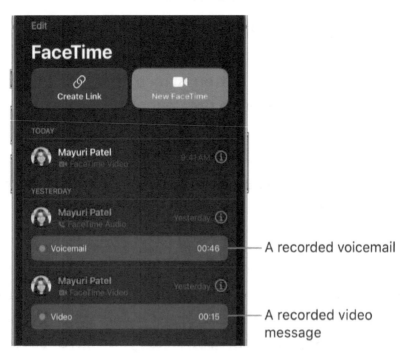

Delete a call from your call history

Enter the FaceTime application, swipe left on a call in your calls history, and touch the **Delete** button.

Create a FaceTime call link

You can create a Face-Time call link & send it to other people, which they can use to participate in the FaceTime call.

❖ Launch the FaceTime application, and then click on the **Create Link** button.

❖ Choose one of the sharing options to send the link.

You can invite anybody to join a Face-Time call even those that don't have Apple devices. They can join the call from their browser, no login is required.

Snap Live Photos in FaceTime calls

While making a video call in the FaceTime application, you can snap a Live Photo. Your iPhone's camera snaps what takes place before and after you capture the picture, including the audio.

To capture Live Photos, first, ensure you've activated Face-Time Live Photos in the Settings application> FaceTime, and then carry out any of the below:

❖ In a call with someone: Touch the Live Photo icon ⬭.
❖ In a Group call: Touch the person's tile, touch the Full Screen icon ⬸, and then touch the Capture icon ⬭

Your iPhone will inform you and the other person that a picture was taken, and the Live Photo will be stored in the Photos application on your device.

Use Live Captions in FaceTime calls

You can activate the **Live Captions** feature in a FaceTime video call to have spoken conversation converted to text and displayed on your iPhone's screen in real time. If you have trouble hearing what is being said in the call, the Live Captions feature can make it easy for you to follow along.

❖ While in a Face-Time video call, touch your screen to display the call controls.

❖ Click the Info button ⓘ, activate Live Captions, and then touch the **Done** button.
Next, a Live Captions window will show the transcribed dialogue and who is speaking.

To disable Live Captions, touch the Info icon ⓘ, and then deactivate Live Captions.

Use another app during a FaceTime call

You can use other applications while on a FaceTime call.

Swipe up from the lower edge of your iPhone's display to show the Home Screen, then touch an app's icon to launch the application.

Touch the green bar in the upper part of your display to go back to the Face-Time screen.

Make a group FaceTime call

In the Face-Time application, you can have about 32 participants in a group call.

❖ Launch the Face-Time app, and then click on the **New FaceTime** button.
❖ Type the phone numbers or names of the persons you want to call in the input field.

Or, click on the Add Contacts button ⊕ to enter the Contacts app and add people from your contacts list.

❖ Touch the FaceTime Video icon ▭◁ to make a video call or the FaceTime Voice Call icon ☎ to make a voice call.

Everyone participating in the call will appear in a tile on your screen. When someone speaks or you tap a tile, that tile will become more prominent.

Add others to a call

Any participant can add someone to a Face-Time call.

❖ While on a FaceTime call, tap your screen to see the call controls, click on the More Information icon ⓘ in the controls, and then click on the **Add People** button.
❖ Type the individual's number, Apple ID, or name in the entry bar.

You can also click on the Add Contacts button ⊕ to add somebody from your contacts list.
❖ Click on the **Add People** button

Leave a Group Face-Time call

Click on the **Leave** button to leave the call.

See participants in a grid layout

While on a FaceTime call with 4 or more individuals, you can choose to see the participants in sizeable tiles arranged in a grid.

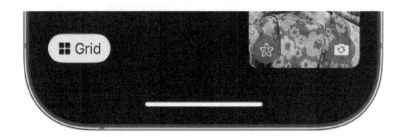

In a Face-Time call, touch the **Grid** button in the lower left corner of your display (touch your screen if the button is not visible).

Touch the **Grid** button once more to deactivate the Grid view.

Share your screen in a Face-Time call

You can share your screen in a FaceTime call to bring sites, applications, and more to the conversation.

❖ While on a FaceTime call, touch the Share Content icon .
❖ Touch the **Share My Screen** button to share your entire screen.
A small image of your display will appear in the Face-Time call after three seconds. The other participants on the call can touch the image to increase its size.

Click on the Stop Sharing Content icon to stop sharing the screen.

Collaborate on a document in a FaceTime call

You can collaborate on shared documents in a Face-Time call.

❖ While on a FaceTime call with individuals you want to work with.

❖ Click the Share Content icon, and then select the application you want to use in the Collaborate Together section.

If you can't find the Share Content button, touch your screen to show the call controls.

❖ Open the document, and then touch the Share icon.

❖ Use one of the sharing options (like Messages, FaceTime, etc.) to share the document with your collaborators in the FaceTime call and then touch the **Collaborate** button.

A notification to start collaborating will appear in the upper part of your display.

❖ Touch the **Start** button, and then click on the **Collaborate** button.

Your collaborators will be notified that you have shared a document. When they touch the **Open** button on the message, the document will open on their device.

Anyone who accepts & opens the document can edit and see changes made by other collaborators. All collaborators are notified of any changes.

Use video effects in video calls

❖ While on a Face-Time video call, swipe down from the upper right corner of your screen to open the Controls Centre.
❖ Click on the **Video Effects** button, then select any of the below:
  ➢ Portrait: This feature will automatically place the focus on you while blurring the background. Click on the More Options icon to change the background blur level

➢ Studio Light: This feature dims the background & brightens your face. Click on the More Options button to change the studio light intensity.

➢ Reactions: This feature allows you to add reactions using hand gestures.

Add reactions in video calls

You can add reactions that fill your screen using basic hand gestures.

You can also add these reactions by long-pressing your tile and then clicking the icons that pop up.

Note: To use hand gestures to add reactions, swipe down from the upper right edge of your screen to open the Controls Center, touch the **Video Effects** button, and ensure **Reactions** is enabled. To show the reactions, simply perform any hand gesture below, and pause for a few seconds for the effect to activate.

Reaction	Gesture	Icon

Balloons

Confetti

Thumbs-down

Laser burst

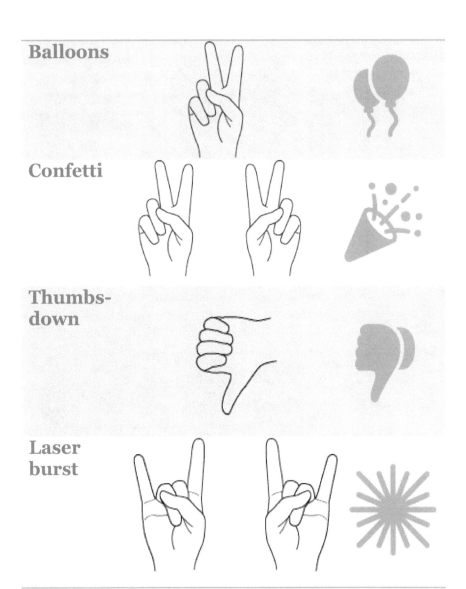

Rain

Firework s

Hearts

Thumbs-up

Switch to back camera

While on a FaceTime call, touch your tile, and then touch the Switch Camera button 📷.

Touch the button 📷, one more time to switch to the front-facing camera.

Turn off the camera

While on a FaceTime call, tap your display to see the call controls, and then click on the Video button 📹. (Touch the button one more time to turn on the camera)

Filter out background noise

You can activate the Voice Isolation feature to prioritize your voice during FaceTime calls and block out background sounds.
While on a Face-Time call, swipe down from the upper right corner of your display to open the

Controls Centre, touch Mic Mode, and then click on the **Voice Isolation** option.

Add the sounds around you

Activate the **Wide Spectrum** feature if you want your voice and the sound around you to be heard in the call.

While on a Face-Time call, swipe down from the upper right corner of your display to open the Controls Centre, touch Mic Mode, and then click on the **Voice Isolation** option.

Turn off the sound

While on a FaceTime call, touch your display to see the call controls if they are not visible, then touch the Mute icon🎤 to mute the sound.

Touch the icon once more to turn on the sound.

Use filters

❖ While on a FaceTime video call, touch your tile, and then touch the Effects icon🌟.
❖ Click the Filters button 🔵 to open the filters.
❖ Touch one of the filters to use it(swipe to preview the filters)

Report FaceTime calls as spam

Swipe left on a call in your FaceTime calls history or in the Recents section in the Phone application, then touch the Report icon ⊙ .

This action will send the caller's info to Apple.

Block unwanted FaceTime callers

❖ In your Face-Time calls history, touch the Info icon ⓘ beside the e-mail address, number, or name of the individual you'd like to block.
❖ Scroll down, click on the **Block this Caller** button, and then touch the **Block Contact** button.

To unblock someone, click on the Info icon ⓘ beside the e-mail address, number, or name of the person in your call log, scroll, and then click on the **Unblock this Caller** button.

BROWSE WITH SAFARI

You can surf the internet using the Safari app.

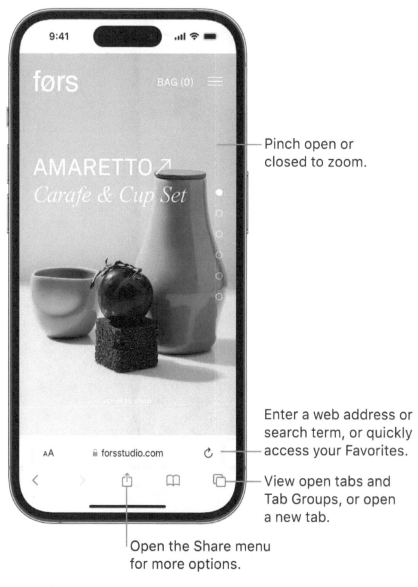

Pinch open or closed to zoom.

Enter a web address or search term, or quickly access your Favorites.

View open tabs and Tab Groups, or open a new tab.

Open the Share menu for more options.

Search the web

❖ Type a word, phrase, or URL in the search box

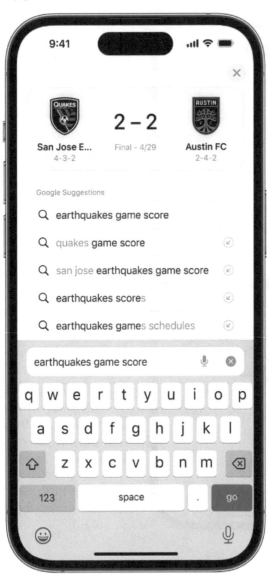

❖ Touch one of the search suggestions, or touch the **Go** key on the onscreen keyboard.

If you do not want to see search suggestions, enter the Settings application, touch Safari, and then disable Search Engine Suggestions.

Surf sites with Safari

You can easily surf through a site in the Safari app.

❖ Return to the top: Double-tap the top edge of your display to quickly go back to the beginning of a very long page.
❖ Rotate your phone to landscape orientation to see more of a webpage
❖ Drag down from the upper edge of a webpage to refresh the page
❖ Share links: Touch the Share icon⬆️ in the lower part of the page.

Preview site links

Long press a link in the Safari application to preview the link without opening the webpage.

Touch the Preview, or touch the **Open** button to open the link.

Touch anywhere outside the preview to close the preview.

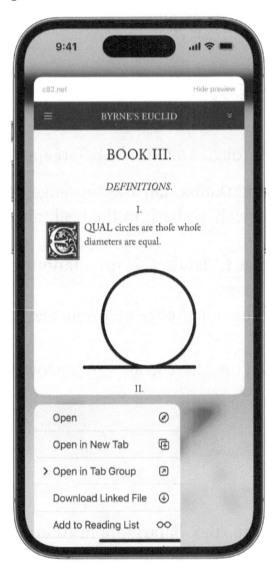

Translate an image or a webpage

When viewing a picture or page that is in a language you don't understand, you can use the Safari browser to translate it.

Click the Page Settings button $A A$, and then click on the Translations icon (if available).

Search a webpage

You can look for a phrase or word on a page.

❖ Touch the Share icon, and then touch the **Find On Page** button.
❖ Type a phrase or word in the search bar
❖ Touch the More Instance icon $\vee$ to go to other mentions.

Choose a search engine

Enter the Settings application, touch Safari, and then touch Search Engine.

Page | 365

Personalize the start page

Any time you open a new tab, it begins on the start page.

- ❖ In the Safari application, touch the Tabs icon ⬓, and then touch the Add icon ＋.
- ❖ Scroll to the end of the page, and then touch the **Edit** button.
- ❖ Select the options you want to appear on the start page:
  - ➢ Favourites.
  - ➢ Frequently Visited
  - ➢ Privacy Report
  - ➢ Shared with you
  - ➢ Reading List
  - ➢ Siri Suggestions
  - ➢ iCloud Tabs
  - ➢ Recently Closed Tabs
  - ➢ Background Image

Change the text size for a site

- ❖ In the Safari application, touch the Page Settings icon A𝖠 in the search field.
- ❖ Touch the big **A** to make the font size bigger or the small **A** to reduce the size.

Change the display controls for a site

❖ In the Safari application, touch the Page Settings icon AA in the search field, and then carry out any of the below:

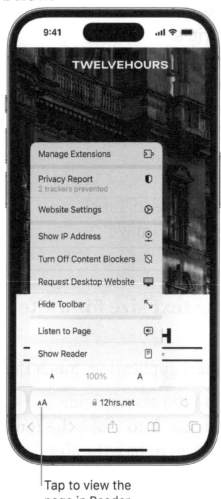

Tap to view the page in Reader.

- ➢ Hide the search box: Touch the **Hide Toolbar** button (touch the lower edge of your display to bring it out).
- ➢ Show a streamlined view of a page: Touch the **Show Reader** button
  Touch the **Hide Reader** button to go back to the normal view.
- ➢ See how the site looks on a computer: Touch the **Request Desktop Site** button.

Change Safari layout on your phone

In Safari, you can choose a tab bar layout that suits your style.

Enter the Settings app, touch Safari, and then scroll to the Tabs section. Choose one of the Tab bar layouts (Single Tab or Tab Bar).

Tabs

You can use tabs to navigate between many open websites.

Open a link in another tab

Long-press the link, and then touch the **Open in New Tab** button.

To remain on the current page anytime you open a new link in another tab, simply enter the Settings application, touch Safari, touch Open Links, and then touch In Background.

See the history of a tab

You can see the websites you've visited in a tab.

Enter the tab, long-press the Back button ‹ or the Forward button ›.

Close tabs

Touch the Tabs icon ⬜, and then touch the Close icon ⊗ in the upper right corner of a tab to close the tab.

Tip: To close every tab in this Tab Group at once, long-press the **Done** button, and then touch the **Close All Tabs** button.

Open a recently closed tab

Touch the Tabs icon , long-press the Add icon╋, and then select from the recently closed tabs list.

Organize tabs with Tab Groups

Create Tab Groups to organize your tabs and make it easy to find them.

Create a new Tab Group

❖ Click the Tabs icon 🗗 to see all your open tabs.
❖ Long-press one of the tabs, and then touch the **Move To Tab Group** button
❖ Touch the **New Tab Group** button, type the name, and then touch the **Move** button.

Tip: To move from one Tab Group to another, click the Tab Groups button ⌄ in the bottom middle of your display.

Rearrange tabs in a Tab Group

❖ Click the Tabs icon 🗗 to see all your open tabs in a Tab Group.
❖ Long-press one of the tabs in the Tab Group
❖ In the menu that pops up, touch the **Arrange Tab By** button, and then select one of the options
You can also drag a tab to any position in the group

Change the name of a Tab Group

❖ Click the Tabs icon 🗗, and then click the Group Tab icon ⌄.

Page | 373

❖ Click on the **Edit** button, and then touch the More Options icon ⊙

❖ Touch the **Rename** button, type another name, and then touch the **Save** button.

Pin a tab to the beginning of a Tab Group

❖ Click the Tabs icon ⬚ to see all your open tabs in the group.

❖ Long-press a tab

❖ Touch the **Pin Tab** button in the menu that pops up.

Move a tab to another Tab Group

❖ Long-press the Tabs icon ⬚ and then touch the **Move to Tabs Group** button.

❖ Select any of the Tab groups you've created or create another group.

Use Siri to listen to a page

You can use Siri to read aloud some websites.

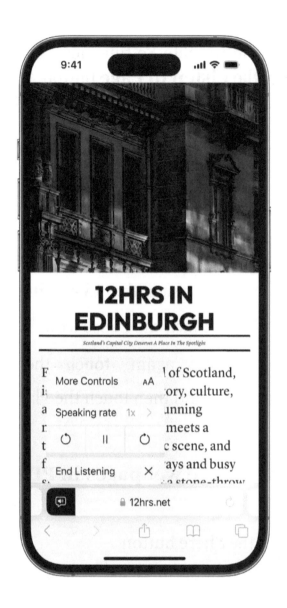

❖ In the Safari application, visit the webpage you'd like to listen to, and then carry out any of the below:

- ➤ Click on the Site Settings icon AA, and then click the **Listen to Page** button.
- ➤ Long-press your iPhone's side button to summon Siri, then say something like " I want to listen to this webpage"

Pause listening

When you're listening to a page, touch the Listening Controls icon 🗨, touch the **Listening Control** button, and then touch the Pause icon ▌▌.

To start listening again, touch the Listening Controls icon 🗨, and then touch the Play icon ▶

Annotate & save webpages in PDF format

- ❖ Click on the Share button ⬆.
- ❖ Click on the Markup icon Ⓐ, and then use the tools to mark up the page.
- ❖ Touch the **Done** button, and then touch the **Save File To** button
- ❖ Select a file, and then touch the **Save** button

Automatically fill in your info in the Safari browser

Use the AutoFill feature to automatically fill in credit cards info & contact info in the Safari browser.

Setup AutoFill

Save your personal info or credit card numbers on your phone to speed up filling out forms online & making purchases.

❖ Enter the Settings application, touch Safari, and then touch AutoFill.
❖ Carry out any of the below:
 ➢ Setup contact information: Activate Use Contacts Info, click on My Info, and then select your contact card. This card's contact information will be entered when you touch the **AutoFill** button on a webpage in the Safari application.
 ➢ Setup credit card information: Activate Credit Card, touch the **Saved Credit Card** button, and then touch the **Add Credit Card** button. Fill in your credit card info into the appropriate fields, or touch the **Use Camera** button to scan your card.

Fill in your contact info automatically

Use the AutoFill feature to quickly add your personal info to forms online.

❖ Touch one of the black fields in a form or site that's compatible with AutoFill in the Safari application.
❖ Touch the **AutoFill Contact** button at the top of your keyboard, and then choose one of the contacts.
❖ You can touch any of the boxes and make adjustments to the info.
❖ Adhere to the directives on your display to submit the form.

Note: You can use the **AutoFill** feature to add other people's info from your contacts list. For instance, if you buy a gift and you are shipping it to a friend; you can use the **AutoFill** feature to fill in their address. Touch the **AutoFill Contact** button, touch the **Other Contacts** button, and then select the person's contact card.

Fill in your credit card info automatically

❖ Touch the credit card info box in a form or site that's compatible with AutoFill in the Safari application.

❖ Touch one of the saved credit cards or touch the **Scan Card** button to capture the front of the card with your camera.

Deactivate AutoFill

Deactivate AutoFill for credit cards or contact info: Enter the Settings application, touch Safari, touch AutoFill, and then deactivate any of the options.

Clear cache on your phone

You can delete your data & history to clear the cache on your phone. This will remove the history of sites you've visited & searched recently on your phone.

❖ In the Safari application, touch the Bookmarks icon ▢.

❖ Click on the History icon ◷, and then touch the **Clear** button.

❖ In the Clear Timeframe section, Select the amount of data you want to delete

❖ Touch the **Clear History** button.

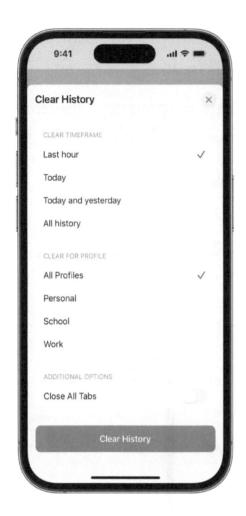

Visit websites privately

In the Private Browsing mode, you can visit websites in private tabs, which will not appear in your browsing history.

If your phone has a passcode, Private Browsing will lock when you aren't using it.

❖ In the Safari application, touch the Tabs icon
❖ Swipe to the right on the tab bar in the lower part of your display till Private Browsing opens, and then click on the **Unlock** button.

To hide the sites & leave private browsing mode, simply touch the Tabs button , and then swipe to the left to open a Tab Group from the menu in the lower part of your screen. Private Browsing will lock automatically, but the sites you've opened will remain open.

To deactivate Private Browsing locking, simply navigate to the Settings app, tap Safari, and then disable the **Require Face ID to Unlock Private Browsing** option or the **Require Passcode to Unlock Private Browsing** option.

Choose a search engine for Private Browsing

Navigate to the Settings app, tap Safari, deactivate the **Also Use in Private Browsing** option, touch Private Search Engine, and then choose one of the options.

PHONE & CONTACTS

To make a phone call in the Phone application, dial the number on the keypad, touch any of your recent calls or favorites, or select any of the phone numbers in your contact list.

Make the call on another line.

Dial a number

❖ Enter the Phone application, and then touch the **Keypad** tab in the lower part of your display.
❖ Carry out any of the below:
  ➢ Use your other line: If your phone is using two SIMs, touch the line in the upper part of your display, and then select one of the lines.
  ➢ Type numbers using the keyboard: Touch the Delete button ✕ to delete any mistake.
  ➢ Redial the last number: Touch the Call button 📞 to see who you last called, then press the Call button 📞 to call that number.
  ➢ Paste a number: Tap the number field at the top, then touch the **Paste** button.
  ➢ Enter a soft pause (2 seconds): Long-press the asterisk (*) button till you see a comma on the input field.
  ➢ Enter a hard pause: Long-press the pound button (#) till you see a semicolon on the input field.
  ➢ Insert "+" for international calls: Long-press the "0" button till you see "+" on the input field.
❖ Touch the Call button 📞 to make a call.

Touch the End Call button  to end the call.

Call your favourites

❖ Enter the Phone application, touch the **Favourites** tab in the lower part of your display, and then select a person to call.
❖ To manage your Favourites list, carry out any of the below:
  ➢ Add someone to your Favourites list: Touch the Add icon ✛, and then choose one of your contacts.
  ➢ Edit or delete favourites: Click on the **Edit** button.

Redial or return recent calls

❖ Enter the Phone application, touch the **Recents** tab, then select one to call.
❖ Click the More Details icon ⓘ to learn more about the call and the caller.

Call one of your contacts

❖ Enter the Phone application, and then touch the **Contacts** tab.
❖ Touch one of your contacts from the list, then touch the phone number you'd like to call.

Activate Dial Assist

When the Dial Assist feature is activated, your phone will automatically determine the correct local or international prefix when you dial. Adhere to the directives below to activate the **Dial Assist** feature:

❖ Enter the Settings application, and touch Phone.
❖ Scroll down and activate the **Dial Assist** feature.

Answer a call

Carry out any of the below:

❖ Touch the Answer button📞.
❖ Drag the slider if your phone is locked.

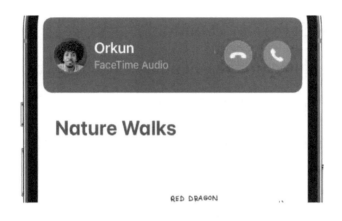

Silence a call

Carry out any of the below:

❖ Press your iPhone's side button
❖ Press one of the volume keys.

You can still answer a call on mute until it disconnects.

Decline a call

Do any of the below:

❖ Double-press your iPhone's side button.
❖ Swipe up on the call banner

❖ Touch the Reject button 🔽 .

Swipe down on the call banner to see more options.

Carry out any of the below:

❖ Touch the **Remind Me** button, then select when you want to be reminded to call the person back.
❖ Touch the **Message** button, and then select one of the default replies or touch the **Custom** button.
To create your default replies, enter the Settings application, touch Phone, touch Respond with Texts, then touch one of the default messages and replace it.

Adjust the volume while on a call

Press the volume buttons to adjust the volume. Swipe down on the call banner and carry out any of the below:

❖ Touch the **Mute** button to mute your device.
❖ Long-press the mute button to place the call on hold.

Use another application during the call

❖ Swipe up from the lower edge of your display to enter your iPhone's Home Screen, then touch an app's icon to open it.
❖ Touch the green indicator in the upper part of your display to go back to the call.

Make a conference call

You can setup a conference call with up to 5 individuals.

❖ During a call, touch the **Add Call** button, call another person, and then touch the **Merge Call** button.
Repeat the steps above to add others to the conference call.
❖ While on a conference call, carry out any of the below:
  ➢ Talk to an individual privately: Click the More Details button ⓘ, and then touch the **Private** button beside the person. Click the **Merge Calls** button to continue the conference call.

- ➢ Add incoming calls on the same line: Touch the Hold Call + Answer button, and then touch the **Merge Calls** button.
- ➢ Drop someone: Click the More Details button ⓘ beside a person, and then touch the **End** button.

Assign a different ringtone to a contact

- ❖ Enter the Contacts application
- ❖ Select one of the contacts from your list, touch the **Edit** button, touch Ringtone, and then choose any of the ringtones.

Block calls and messages from certain persons

- ❖ Enter the Phone application, and then touch the Favourites, Voicemail, or Recent button.
- ❖ Click the More Details button ⓘ beside the contact or phone number you plan on blocking, scroll down, and then touch the **Block this Caller** button.

Manage your blocked contacts

❖ Enter the Settings application, touch Phone, and then touch Blocked Contacts.
❖ Touch the **Edit** button.

Create a contact

Launch the Contacts app, touch the Add icon $+$, and then fill in your contact details.

Find a contact

Launch the Contacts app, touch the search field, and then type a number, name, or any other contact info.

Share contacts

Launch the Contacts app, touch one of the contacts, click on the **Share Contact** button, and then select a sharing option.

Delete a contact

❖ Launch the Contacts app, touch a contact, and then click on the **Edit** button.
❖ Scroll down and then touch the **Delete Contact** button.

Quickly reach a contact

In the Contacts application, touch one of the contacts, and then touch one of the buttons under the name of the contact to start a message, make a call, and more.

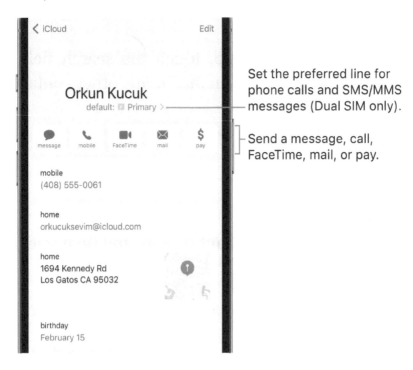

Edit contacts

In Contacts, you can assign a picture to one of your contacts, add a date of birth, & more.

❖ Touch one of the contacts in the Contacts app, and then click on the **Edit** button

* ❖ Enter or change the contact's details
* ❖ Touch the Done button to save the changes.

Add or edit your poster & picture

You can set a poster & picture to appear automatically when you call or send messages to other people. To do this, simply adhere to the directives below:

* ❖ Enter the Contacts application, touch the **My Card** button at the top of the list, and then click on Contact Photos & Posters.
* ❖ (Optional) touch the **Name** fields, and enter the name you want others to see, then touch the **Edit** button to select a poster or create one for yourself.
* ❖ Scroll down and activate Name & Photo Sharing to start sharing your poster & picture with other people.

Complete or edit My Card

Use My Card to easily share your info with other people

❖ Enter the Contacts application, touch My Card at the top of the list, and then touch the **Edit** button
❖ Insert your contact info

If you can't find **My Card**, touch the Add icon ✛ and fill in your info, then go back to the contact list, long-press your contact, and touch the **Make this My Card** button.

Use NameDrop to share your contact details with new people

NameDrop allows iPhone users to easily share their contact details with nearby iPhones. Adhere to the directives below to use the NameDrop feature:

❖ Put the top of your phone close to the top of another iPhone to share your contact info.
A light from the top of both devices lights up to indicate a connection. Keep holding & NameDrop will appear on the two screens.

❖ You and the other person can now select any of the options below:

  ➤ **Share**: Receive the other individual's contact details and share yours too
  If you are sharing your contact info, touch the Options icon ❯ , choose the fields you want to add, and then touch the **Save** button. These fields will be preselected the next time you use NameDrop.

  ➤ **Receive Only**: Receive the other person's contact details.

To cancel the process, move both devices away from each other before Name-Drop completes.

Note: To deactivate the NameDrop feature, enter the Settings application, touch General, touch AirDrop, and then deactivate the **Bring Devices Together** feature.

Save a number you just dialed

❖ In the Phone application, touch the Keypad tab in the lower part of the screen, type a number, and then touch the **Add Number** button.
❖ Touch the **Create a New Contact** button, or the **Add to an Existing Contacts** option, and then select one of the contacts.

Add recent callers to contacts

❖ Open the Phone application, click on the **Recents** tab in the lower part of the screen, and then click on the More Information icon ⓘ beside the number.

❖ Click on the **Create a New Contact** button, or the **Add to an Existing Contacts** option, and then choose one of the contacts.

MAIL

In the Mail application, you can write, send, & schedule e-mails.

Change mailboxes or accounts.

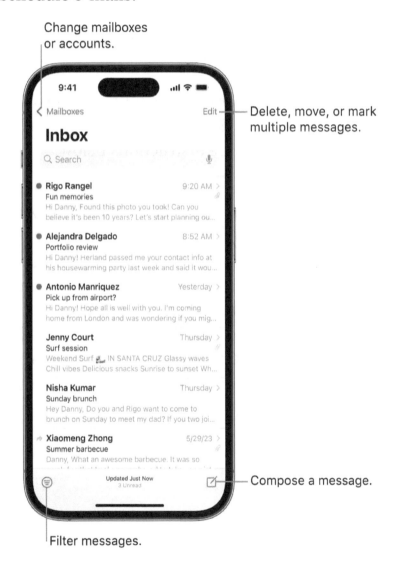

Delete, move, or mark multiple messages.

Compose a message.

Filter messages.

Add email accounts

Before you can start sending & receiving e-mails through the Mail application, you must first add the email account you want to use. The 1st time you launch the Mail app on your iPhone, you'll be asked to setup an e-mail account.

You can add more email accounts to the Mail application from the Settings application. To do this, simply adhere to the instructions below:

❖ Enter the Settings app, and tap Mail
❖ Click on Accounts, and then click the **Add Account** button
❖ Touch one of the email services—for instance, Gmail or iCloud—and then insert your e-mail account details in the appropriate fields.
   If you can't find the e-mail service you are using in the list, touch **Other**, touch the **Add Mail Account** button, and then fill in your e-mail account details.

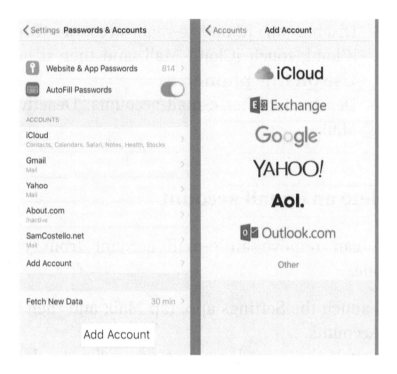

Temporarily stop making use of an e-mail account

You can deactivate an e-mail account in the Settings app if you want to stop using it. You can easily reactivate it at anytime.

❖ Launch the Settings app, tap Mail, and then tap Accounts.
❖ Touch the e-mail account you'd like to deactivate, and then carry out any of the below:

Page | 403

➤ Disable an iCloud e-mail account: Touch iCloud, touch iCloud Mail, and then disable **Use on this phone**.
➤ Deactivate other e-mail accounts: Deactivate Mail.

Delete an e-mail account

You can remove an e-mail account from your phone.

❖ Launch the Settings app, tap Mail, and then tap Accounts.
❖ Touch the e-mail account you'd like to delete from your phone, and then click on Delete Account or Sign Out.

Read an email

Launch the Mail app, and tap one of the e-mails in the inbox.

Use the Remind Me feature to come back to e-mails later

If there is no time to handle an email at the moment, you can set a time & date to get a reminder and bring the message to the beginning of your inbox.

Touch the Reply icon ↰, touch the **Remind Me** button, and select the reminder time.

Preview an e-mail & more

You can preview an e-mail to see its content without completely opening the email. In the inbox, press & hold an e-mail to preview its content and view a list of options for forwarding, muting, etc.

Provide longer preview for each email

In your inbox, the Mail app shows two lines by default for each e-mail. You can choose to see more lines of text when you preview an e-mail.

Enter the Settings application, touch Mail, touch Preview, and then select up to 5 lines.

Write an email message

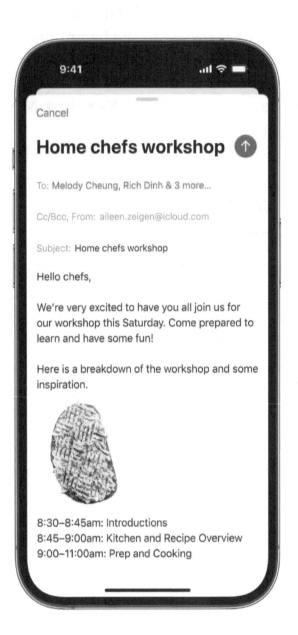

- ❖ Launch the Mail app, and then tap the Compose icon ☑.
- ❖ Tap in the email, and then write what you want.
- ❖ To change the format, touch the Tools Extension icon ‹ at the top of the keyboard, and then touch the Text Format icon Aa.
  You can use one of the different font styles & text colours; you can also add numbered or bulleted lists.
- ❖ Touch the Send icon ⬆ to send the e-mail.

Add recipients

- ❖ Touch the To field, then type the recipients' names.
  While typing, the Mail application will automatically suggest individuals from your Contact list.

  You can also touch the Add Contact icon ⊕ to enter the Contacts app and add people from your contacts list.
- ❖ If you'd like to send a copy to others, touch the Cc/ Bcc field and then do any of the below:

- ➢ Touch the Cc box, and then type the names of the persons you want to send a copy to.
- ➢ Touch the Bcc box, and then type the names of the persons you do not want other recipients to see.

Schedule an email with the Send Later feature

Press & hold the Send button⬆, and then select when you want the email to be sent.

Click on the **Send Later** button to view more options.

Send an e-mail from another account

If you have multiple e-mail accounts, you can choose the account you want to send an e-mail from.

- ❖ In your e-mail draft, touch the Cc /Bcc, From field.
- ❖ Touch the From Field, and then choose one of your accounts.

Unsend an e-mail

The Undo Send feature allows you to unsend an e-mail in the Mail application.

You have about ten seconds to change your mind after sending an e-mail.

Click on the **Undo Send** button in the lower part of the inbox to unsend the e-mail.

Delay sending e-mails

You can give yourself more than 10 seconds to change your mind and unsend emails. To do this, simply head over to the Settings app, click Mail, click on **Undo Send Delay**, and then choose one of the options.

Reply to an email

❖ Tap in the e-mail, touch the Reply button ↩, and then do any of the below:
  ➢ Reply to the sender: Touch the **Reply** button.
  ➢ Reply to the sender and others: Touch the **Reply All** button
❖ Write your message

Forward an e-mail to new recipients

❖ Tap in the e-mail, touch the Reply button ↩,
and then touch the **Forward** button.
If the original e-mail contains attachments such
as pictures or documents, you can decide
whether or not to include them in the e-mail.
Select the **Include** or **Don't Include** option.
❖ Insert the e-mail address of the recipients.
❖ Tap in the e-mail, then write what you want. The
forwarded message is shown below.

Follow up on e-mails

If you send an e-mail and don't get a response for a
few days, the e-mail will automatically move back
to the top of your inbox so you don't forget to follow
up.

To deactivate this feature, enter the Settings app,
touch Mail, and then deactivate Follow-Up
Suggestions.

Attach photos, videos, or documents to email

You can add a picture, video, & document in your e-mail for recipients to download and store on their device.

❖ Touch where you want to add the attachment in the e-mail, and then tap on the Expand Tools button ❮ at the top of your keyboard.

❖ Carry out any of the below:

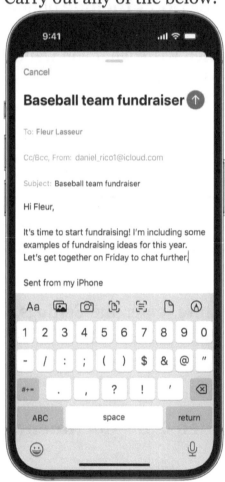

➤ Add a document: Click on the Insert Attachments button⬜ at the top of your keyboard, then look for the file in the Files app.
In the Files app, touch the **Recents**, **Browse**, or **Shared** button in the lower part of your screen, then touch a location, or one of the folders or files to open it.

➤ Add a saved video or picture: Touch the Insert Photos button🖼 at the top of the keyboard, and then select one of the photos or videos. Click on the Close icon ✕ to go back to the e-mail.

➤ Record a video or capture a picture & add it to the e-mail: Touch the Capture icon📷 at the top of your keyboard, and then capture a picture or record a video. Touch the **Use Video** or **Use Photo** button to add the file to your e-mail, or touch the **Retake** button if you want to take another shot.

Scan & add a document to an e-mail

You can scan a document and send it in PDF format.

❖ Touch where you want to add the scanned file in your email, and then click on the Expand Tools button ‹ at the top of your keyboard.

❖ Touch the Scan Document icon 🗋 at the top of the keyboard.

❖ Set your phone in a way that the document can be seen clearly on your screen—your device will automatically capture the page.
To manually capture the document, touch the White Shutter ○. Click on the Flashlight button ⚡ to turn the flashlight on or off.

❖ Touch the **Keep Scan** or the **Retake** button, scan more pages, and then touch the **Save** button when you are done.

❖ To edit the saved scanned, tap it, and then carry out any of the below:

➢ Touch the Crop icon 🗘 to crop the photo.

➢ Click on the Show Filters icon ● to use one of the filters.

➢ Click the Rotate icon ◻ to rotate the file.

➢ Touch the Delete icon 🗑 to delete the scanned file

Create & attach a drawing to your e-mail

You can draw in emails to express ideas that are difficult to express in words. The drawing will be attached to the e-mail as an attachment.

❖ Touch where you want to add the scanned file in your email, and then click on the Expand Tools button ⟨ at the top of your keyboard.
❖ Touch the Markup icon Ⓐ to see the Markup tools panel.
❖ Pick any of the drawing tools & colours, then use your finger to draw or write.
❖ When you are done, simply touch the **Done** button, and then touch the **Insert Drawing** button.

To continue working on a drawing, touch the drawing in the e-mail, and then touch the Markup icon Ⓐ.

Download email attachments sent to you

Long-press the attachment, then touch the **Save to Files** button or the **Save Image** button.

If you pick the **Save Image** option, you can look for the file in the Photos application. If you pick the **Save to Files** option, you can find the file in the Files application.

Tip: To open the attachment with any other application, click on the **Share** button and then select any of the applications.

Quickly fill out forms received in the Mail application

Use the **AutoFill** feature to quickly fill out forms you receive in the Mail application, and then send them to the original sender without leaving the Mail application (iOS 17.20 or after).

❖ Touch the attachment in the email to open the document.

❖ Click the AutoFill button ⌨️ , and then touch an empty field to enter text.

❖ To enter text in another line, simply touch it and insert text.

❖ Touch the **Done** button, and then touch **Reply to** [name].

Annotate email attachment

In the Mail application, you can write & draw on a PDF attachment, picture, or video, then store it on your device or send it back.

❖ Touch the attachment in the e-mail, and then click on the Markup icon Ⓐ .

❖ Select any of the drawing tools, and use your finger to draw.

❖ When you are done, touch the **Done** button, and then select one of the options on your display.

Setup email notifications

You can change your e-mail notification settings in the Mail application.

Mute e-mail notifications

To reduce the interruption of active emails, you can turn off notifications from a message.

❖ Open an e-mail
❖ Click on the Reply icon ↩, then click the **Mute** button.

To specify what you want to happen to e-mails you mute, enter the Settings application, touch Mail, touch Muted Thread Action, and then choose one of the options.

Change your email notification settings

❖ Enter the Settings application, touch Mail, touch Notifications, and enable Allow Notifications.
❖ Touch the **Customize Notifications** button, then touch the e-mail account you want to change.
❖ Choose the settings you want, such as Badges Alerts.

Email filtering on iPhone

You can use filters to quickly display messages that match any criteria you choose in the filter list. For instance, if you choose "Mail with Attachments Only", you'll only see e-mails that have attachments.

❖ Touch the Filters icon ⬡ in the mailbox list.

Filter messages.

❖ Touch the "**Filtered by**" button, and then choose or activate the criteria for the e-mails you want to see.

Touch the Filters icon⬤ to deactivate all filters. To disable a certain filter, click on the **"Filtered by"** button, and then unselect it.

Match a mail account to a Focus mode

You can choose which e-mail account receives notifications when a Focus mode is activated. For instance, you can set filters to only display your work e-mail account and notifications from that account when you activate Work Focus.

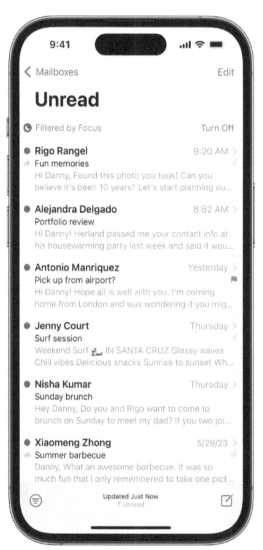

❖ Enter the Settings application, touch Focus, and then touch one of the Focus modes.
❖ Touch the **Add Filter** button under Focus Filters, then touch Mail
❖ Select the accounts you want to appear in your mailbox when the Focus mode is activated.

Search for an email in the Mail application

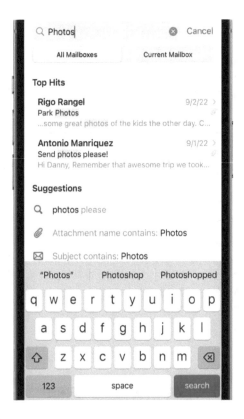

❖ In the mailbox, drag down to show the search box, touch it, and then type the text you want.
❖ Touch Current Mailbox or All Mailboxes.
❖ Touch the **Search** button, and then touch any of the e-mails that appear in the results list to open it.

Manage email with a swipe

When viewing your e-mail list, you can perform different actions by simply swiping an email. Carry out any of the below:

❖ To open an actions list, slowly swipe left on an e-mail until you see the actions menu, then touch one of the items.
❖ Drag the email to the right to show other actions.
❖ Swipe all the way to the left to use the rightmost action.

To choose the action you want to appear in the menu, simply enter the Settings application, touch Mail, touch Swipe Options in the Messages List section, and then select from the available options.

Organize your mail with mailboxes

You can view any of the mailboxes, organize them, create new ones, and more.

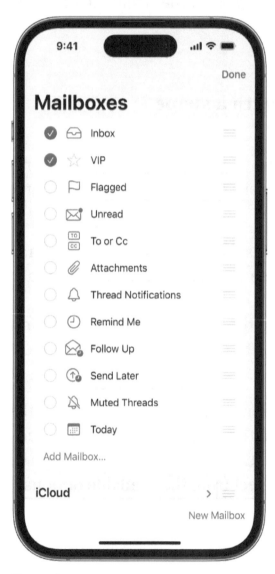

To organize your mailbox, click the Back button ❮ till you see Mailboxes. Click on the **Edit** button, and then carry out any of the below:

❖ View mailboxes: Select the checkboxes beside the mailboxes you'd like to see in the mailbox list.

❖ Rearrange mailboxes: Long-press the Organize button ☰ beside a mailbox till it lifts up, and then drag the mailbox to another position in the list.

❖ Create a mailbox: Click on the **New-Mailbox** button, and then adhere to the directives on your screen.

❖ Change the name of a mailbox: Touch the mailbox, and then touch the name. Erase the name, and then type another one.

❖ Delete a mailbox: Touch the mailbox, and then touch the **Delete Mailbox** button.

Check e-mails from one account at a time

If you have more than one email account in the Mail application, you can use the mailbox list to view e-mails from one account at a time.

Click the Back button ❮ till you see Mailboxes, then touch the mailbox under the e-mail account you want to open.

Each mailbox that appears under a specific e-mail account shows e-mail from that e-mail account only. For instance, to view email sent only from your iCloud account, touch the **iCloud** button, and then touch the **Sent** button.

Move an e-mail to Junk

To move an e-mail to the Junk folder, open the e-mail, click on the Reply icon ↩, and then touch the **Move to Junk** button.

Use Mail Privacy Protection

Activate the Mail Privacy Protection feature to make it very difficult for senders to get info about your Mail activities. To protect your e-mail privacy, the **Mail Privacy Protection** feature hides your IP address from senders, so that they cannot link it to your other online activities or pinpoint your location. It also stops e-mail senders from knowing if you have opened the e-mail they sent.

❖ Launch the Settings app, touch Mail, and then touch Privacy Protection.
❖ Activate Protect Mail Activities.

Delete e-mails

There are different ways to delete e-mails. Carry out any of the below:

❖ Touch the Delete button 🗑 while viewing an email.
❖ While going through your e-mail list, swipe left on one of the e-mails, then click on the **Trash** button.

❖ Delete many e-mails at the same time: While surfing through your e-mail list, click on the **Edit** button, touch the e-mails you'd like to delete, and then click on the **Trash** button.

Recover deleted emails

❖ Keep touching the Back icon ‹ till you see Mailboxes.

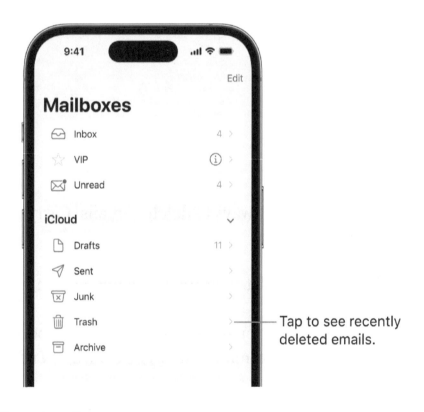

❖ Click on the **Trash** icon 🗑, touch the e-mail you'd like to recover, and then click on the Reply button ↰.

❖ Click the **Move Message** button, and then pick another mailbox.

Print Email

In an e-mail, click on the Reply icon ↰, and then touch the **Print** button.

Print a photo or attachment

Touch an attachment to open it, touch the Share icon ⬆, and then click on the **Print** button.

TRANSLATE

You can use the Translate application to translate conversations, text, & audio from another language to a language you understand.

Translate your voice or text

❖ Launch the Translate application
❖ Touch the language you'd like to translate the selected text to.

Click on the Swap button ↻ to swap languages.
❖ Touch any of the below:

➤ Translate your voice: Touch the Listen icon 🎤, and then speak.
➤ Translate text: Touch **Enter text**, type what you would like to translate (or paste a copied text), and then click on the **Next** button on the keyboard.
You can also touch the **Done** button in the upper left part of your display.
❖ When the translated text appears, carry out any of the below:

➤ Touch the Play button ▶ to play the audio translation.

Press & hold the Play button ▶ to change the playback speed rate

➤ Touch the Full Screen icon ⤢ to display the translated text in full screen.

➢ Click on the Copy button 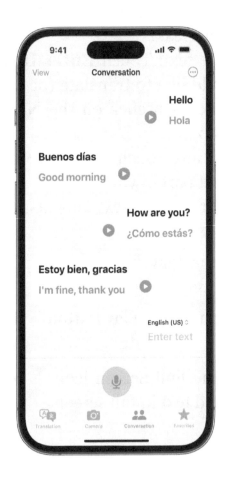 to copy the translated text.

Swipe the translation down to show your recent history.

Translate a conversation

❖ Touch the **Conversation** tab in the lower part of your display
❖ Tap on any of the below:
  ➢ Translate your voice: Touch the Listen button 🎤 , and then speak.
  ➢ Enter Text: Touch **Enter text,** type what you want to translate, and then touch the **Done** button
❖ Touch the "Play" button ▶ to listen to the translation.
   You can set your iPhone to automatically play the audio translation, to do this, simply click on the More Options button ⋯ , and then click on the **Play Translations** button

You can translate a discussion without having to tap the MIC button before each person talks. Touch the More Options button ⋯ , touch the **Auto-Translate** button, and then touch the Listen button 🎤 to begin the discussion. Your phone will automatically detect when you start & stop speaking.

When having a face-to-face conversation, click on the **View** button in the upper left part of the screen, and then click on the **Face-to-Face** button so that everybody can see the chat from their side.

Review words that have multiple meanings

When you translate words that have multiple meanings, you can choose the meaning you want. You can also choose masculine or feminine translations for words with grammatical gender variations.

❖ Enter the Translate application.
❖ Translate a phrase or word, and then touch the **Next** button on your keyboard.
❖ If available, carry out any of the below:
  ➢ Pick another meaning: If available, touch the light-coloured word to choose a different meaning.
  ➢ Select a grammatical gender translation: If available, touch the light-coloured word to choose a masculine or feminine translation.

To deactivate grammatical gender translations, touch the More Options icon ⊙, and then touch the **Show Grammatical Gender** button.

Download languages for offline translation

❖ Navigate to the Settings app, and then touch **Translate**.

❖ Carry out any of the below:
  ➢ Touch the **Downloaded Language** button, and then touch the Download button close to the language you plan on downloading.
  ➢ Enable On-Device Mode

MAPS

You can see your location on a map and zoom in to find the needed details in the Maps app.

Allow the Maps application to use your location

To find your location & get correct directions, your phone has to be connected to the internet via WiFi or mobile network and Precise Location has to be enabled.

❖ If the Maps application shows a message stating that Location Services is disabled: Touch the message, touch Turn On in Setting, and then activate Location Service.
❖ If the Maps application shows a message that Precise Location is disabled: Touch the message, touch Turn On in Setting, touch the **Location** button, and then enable the **Precise Location** feature.

Show where you are on the map

Touch the Locate button ⌁ .

You will see your location in the centre of the map. The top of the map is the North. If you want the Maps app to show where you are heading at the top instead of north, simply click on the Headings icon

✔. Touch the Direction Control icon ⋏ or the Compass icon ᴺ to start showing north.

Select the correct map

The icon in the upper-right part of a map shows whether the map is for driving🚗, satellite view🌀, transport🚊 or sightseeing▮▮▮. Adhere to the guidelines below to use another type of map:

❖ Click on the icon in the upper right corner of the screen.
❖ Pick any other type of map, and then touch the Close icon ✕ .

View a 3D map

Do any of the below on a 2D map:

❖ Swipe up with 2 of your fingers.
❖ Touch the 3D button in the upper right corner of a Satellite map.

❖ In some cities, touch the 3D button in the upper right part of the screen.

You can carry out any of the below on a 3D map:

❖ Drag 2 of your fingers down or up to change the angle.
❖ Zoom in to view buildings & other small features.
❖ Touch the **2D** button in the upper right corner of your display to go back to a 2D map.

Move, zoom, or rotate a map or globe

❖ Drag a map in the Maps application to move around it.
❖ Zoom in or out: Pinch open on a map to zoom in on it. Pinch closed on the map to zoom out
❖ Rotate a map: Long-press the map with 2 of your fingers, and then rotate your fingers.
After rotating the map, touch the Compass icon
   to display north at the upper part of your screen
❖ Explore the world with a 3D globe: Zoom out on the map continuously until it turns to a globe.

Drag the map to move around it, or zoom in to find details for oceans, mountains, etc.

Download offline maps on your device

You can save a location in the Maps app so that you can easily use it when your phone does not have an internet connection.

Change the size of
the map to download.

❖ Launch the Maps application.
❖ Carry out any of the below:
  ➢ Long-press the map till a pin marker pops up
    on your display, then touch the **Download**
    button.
  ➢ Touch your photo or initials beside the search
    box, and then click on **Offline Maps**, click

the **Download New Map** button, and then type a location in the search box, or click on the **Current Location** button.
❖ Select a region, and then touch the **Download** button.

Open or edit a map you have downloaded

❖ Launch the Maps application.
❖ Touch your initials or photo beside the search box, and then click on the **Offline Maps** button.

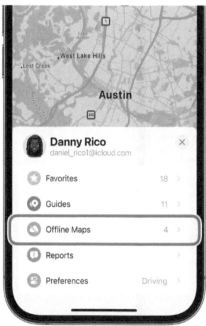

❖ Carry out any of the below:

- ➤ Touch the map's name to open it.
- ➤ Change the map's name: Swipe left on the map, and then touch the **Rename** button.
- ➤ Change the area covered by the map: Click the name of the map, and then click on the **Resize** button on the map's image.

Change your offline map settings

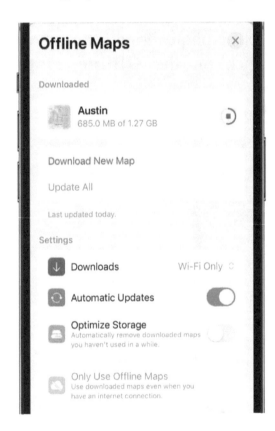

After downloading a map for offline use, you can change the settings—such as when to download or update the map.

❖ Launch the Maps application on your device.
❖ Touch your initials or photo beside the search box, and then click on the **Offline Maps** button.
❖ Scroll & select the settings you'd like to adjust.

Find places on iPhone with Maps

Touch the search box, then type a location.

You can search in different ways. For instance:

❖ Area ("Damascus Town")
❖ Business (restaurants in Toronto, movies, and more.)
❖ Intersections ("9th & Market")
❖ ZIP Code ("69399")
❖ Landmark (Statue of Liberty)

Touch any of the results in the list to get more details about the place or receive directions to the place.

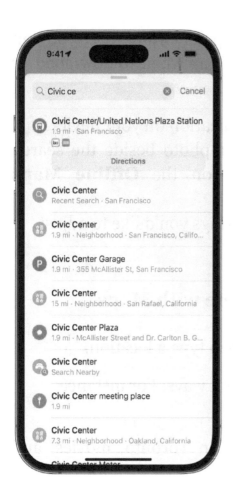

Find nearby attractions, restaurants, or services

Touch the search box, and then carry out any of the below:

❖ Type something like parks or playground in the search box, and then click on the "See Nearby" result.

❖ Click any of the categories such as Restaurant or Grocery Store in the **Find Nearby** segment of the card

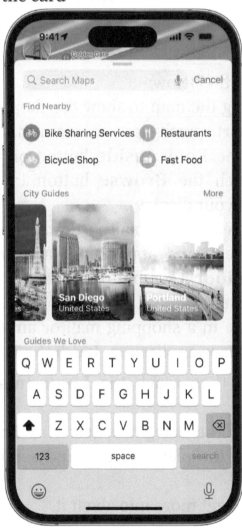

You can also long-press the Maps application icon on your iPhone's Home Screen, and then touch the **Search Nearby** button.

Find your way around a shopping mall or airport

❖ Carry out any of the below:
- ➤ Zoom in: Drag the map to show the shopping mall or airport, pinch open to zoom in, and then touch the **Look Inside** button on the map (or touch the **Browse** button in the lower part of your display).
- ➤ Use search: Search for an airport or shopping center in the Maps application, and then touch the **Indoor Map** button if you see it in the search results.
- ➤ When you are in a shopping mall or airport: Launch the Maps application, touch the Track icon⍋, and then touch the **Look Inside** button.

❖ Click on one of the categories (such as Food, Toilets, etc.) on the place card to find services that are nearby.

Touch a result to get more info about it.

❖ To see a map of another floor, click on the button showing the floor level (pinch open to zoom in if the button is not visible).

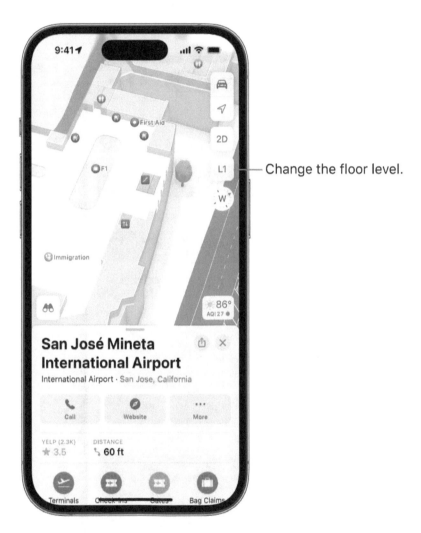

Change the floor level.

Note: The Indoor map is only available for some malls & airports.

APPLE PAY

You can use Apple Pay to safely pay for items in stores, applications, & sites that support Apple Pay.

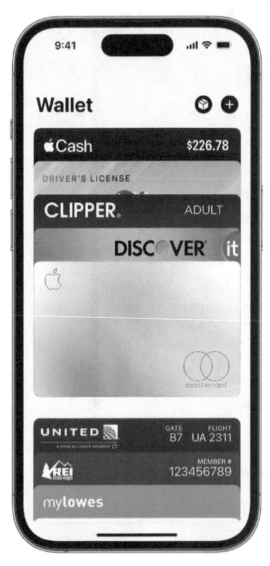

Add a debit or credit card

❖ Launch the Wallet application, and then touch the Add button ⊕. You may be prompted to log in using your Apple ID.
❖ Carry out any of the below:
  ➢ Add a new card: Touch Credit or Debit Card, touch the **Continue** button, and then set your card in a way that its details can be seen clearly on the camera screen, or simply fill in the card info manually.
  ➢ Add your old card: Touch the **Previous Cards** button, and then choose a card that you've used before. These cards can include cards that you've removed, cards that are associated with your Apple ID, and more. Touch the **Continue** button, confirm with Face ID, and then adhere to the instructions on the screen.
  ➢ Add cards from your bank or card issuer's application: Touch your card issuer or bank's application in the **From Apps on Your iPhone** section.

Your card provider will determine whether your card is qualified for Apple Pay & might ask you for more details to finish the verification process.

View a card info & change its settings

❖ Launch the Wallet application, and then touch any of your cards.

❖ Touch the More Options button⊙, and then touch any of the below:
  ➢ Card Details: View more info; change payment address; enable or disable transactions history; or remove the card from the Wallet app.
  ➢ Card number.
  ➢ Notifications: Enable or disable notifications

Link your account to the Wallet app

With compatible card issuers, you can link your account to the Wallet application. After linking your account, you can check your account balance, complete transactions history, etc. in the Wallet application.

❖ Launch the Wallet application.
❖ Touch the card you'd like to connect
❖ Touch the **Get Started** button, and then adhere to the directives on your display to connect your account.

If you can't find the **Get Started** button under a card, it means your card provider does not support this feature.

Find places that accept Apple Pay

You can use Apple Pay for secure, contactless payments in restaurants, stores, & etc.

You can use Apple Pay anywhere you see the following payment logos:

Pay for items with the default card

❖ Press your iPhone's side button twice quickly.
❖ When you see your default card, stare at your phone to confirm with Face ID or insert your iPhone's passcode.

❖ Put the top of your phone close to the card reader and wait till Done & a confirmation icon appear on your display.

Pay with another card

❖ Press your iPhone's side button twice quickly.

❖ When your phone shows your default card, touch it, and then pick one of your other cards
❖ Stare at your iPhone screen to verify with Face ID or insert your phone's passcode.
❖ Put the top of your phone close to the card reader and wait till Done & a confirmation icon appear on your display.

Use Apple Pay in applications, Applications Clips, and Safari

You can use Apple Pay to make payments for items you purchase in applications, Application Clips, & online using the Safari browser.

❖ When checking out, touch the **Apple Pay** button.
❖ Go through your payments info and set any of the below:
  ➢ Contact info
  ➢ Shipping & Billing Address
  ➢ Credit card
  ➢ Amount & frequency of recurring payments.
❖ Press your iPhone's side button twice quickly, and then stare at your phone to confirm with Face ID or type your iPhone's passcode.

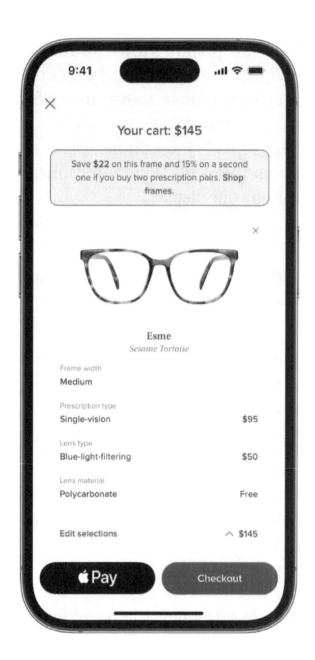

9:41

Your cart: $145

Save **$22** on this frame and 15% on a second one if you buy two prescription pairs. **Shop frames.**

×

Esme
Sesame Tortoise

Frame width
Medium

Prescription type
Single-vision $95

Lens type
Blue-light-filtering $50

Lens material
Polycarbonate   Free

Edit selections   ∧ $145

 Pay   Checkout

Change your information

❖ Enter the Settings app, and touch Wallet & Apple Pay.
❖ Set any of the below:
  ➢ E-mail
  ➢ Shipping address
  ➢ Phone

Change your Apple Pay settings

❖ Enter the Settings app, and touch Wallet & Apple Pay.
❖ Carry out any of the below:
  ➢ Double-press the Side Button: Press your iPhone's side button twice quickly to see your passes & cards on your display.
  ➢ Allow payments on your MacOS device: Allows your phone to authenticate payments on your nearby MacOS device.

Remove cards in the Wallet app

❖ Enter the Wallet application, touch the card you'd like to remove, and then touch the More Options icon ⊙ or the Info icon ⓘ
❖ Touch the **Remove Card** button

JOURNAL

The Journal application (iOS 17.20) makes getting into the habit of journaling easy. Journaling suggestions organize workouts, pictures, outings, etc. to help you recall & reflect on those experiences. You can also lock the application so that only you can gain access to the app.

Setup the Journal app

When you launch the Journal application for the first time, simply adhere to the directives on your display to activate and personalize journal suggestions.

Create a journal entry

❖ Launch the Journal application.
❖ Click on the Add icon ⊕.
❖ Touch the **New Entry** button, or select one of the journaling suggestions or reflection prompts. (If you've deactivated Journaling Suggestions, you can simply start writing.)

Tip: To save a suggestion for later, simply long-press it, and then touch the **Save Without Writing** button.

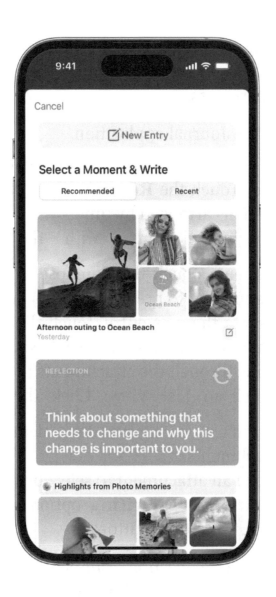

Use journaling suggestions

Journaling suggestions organize workouts, pictures, outings, etc. to help you recall & reflect on those experiences.

- ❖ Enter the Journal application.
- ❖ Click the Edit button ⊕, and see the options offered. Touch the **Recents** button to show the suggestions arranged by time.
- ❖ To begin an entry with the suggested attachments, touch the Compose icon ☑ in the suggestion. Or, to preview the attachment before you create the new entry, touch the suggestion, and then carry out any of the below:
  - ➢ Swipe through the attachments to view them.
  - ➢ Switch to List View: Click the List View button ☰ to view the details of all attachments.
  - ➢ Touch an attachment to select or unselect it.
- ❖ Touch the **Start Writing** option or the **Save Without Writing** button

To delete a suggestion, simply long-press the suggestion, and then touch the **Remove** button.

Add information to an entry

While entering text, you can:

❖ Change the date: Click the More Options icon ,
  and then select another date.

- ❖ Receive suggestions from your recent activities: Touch the Smart Suggestions icon, touch the **Recents** button, and then choose from the different options.
- ❖ Add videos & pictures from the photo library: Touch the Photos button at the top of your keyboard, then select from the ones on your library.
- ❖ Record a voice note: Touch the Voice icon.
- ❖ Touch the Camera icon to snap a picture or record a video.
- ❖ Add a map location: Touch the Track icon, then type a location or select one of the suggested locations. To change the location, touch the thumb-nail, and then touch the Edit icon.
- ❖ Touch the thumbnail of an attachment to show it in full screen.
- ❖ Rearrange attachments by long-pressing a thumbnail, and then dragging it to another position.
- ❖ Touch the Remove icon in the thumbnail to remove an attachment.

Start a journal entry from a different application

When you are using other apps—like playing songs in the Music application or reading articles in the News application—you can still quickly capture your ideas.

❖ In the application you are using, touch the **Share** button or the Share icon ⬆, then touch the **Journal** button. (If you can't find Journal in the list, you might have to add it to your sharing options.)
❖ Enter what you have in mind, and then touch the **Save** button.

Review your old journal entries

The Journal application provides a customizable view of your entries.

View & filter your journal entries

❖ Launch the Journal application.
❖ Scroll to see your past entries.

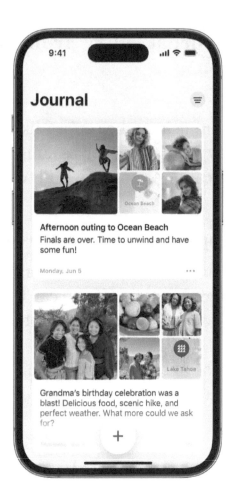

❖ Touch the text in one of the entries to expand the entry. Touch it once more to collapse the entry. Touch any of the attachments to show it in full screen.

❖ To only show certain types of entries, touch the Filter icon ≡, and then select one of the categories.

Bookmark entries

❖ Launch the Journal application.
❖ Carry out any of the below:
  ➢ Click the More Options icon •••, and then click the **Bookmarks** button.
  ➢ Long-press any entry, and then touch the **Bookmark** button.
  ➢ Swipe right on any of the entries, and then touch the Bookmark icon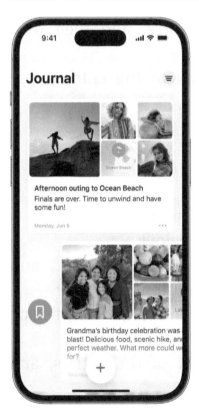

❖ If you want to see only the entries you've bookmarked, touch the Filter icon ☰ , and then touch the **Bookmarked** button.

Edit an entry

❖ Launch the Journal application.
❖ Carry out any of the below:
  ➢ Click the More Options icon •••, and then click the **Edit** button.
  ➢ Long-press any entry, and then touch the **Edit** button.
  ➢ Swipe left on any of the entries, and then touch the Edit icon ✎

Delete an entry

❖ Launch the Journal application.
❖ Carry out any of the below:
  ➢ Click the More Options icon •••, and then click the **Delete** button.
  ➢ Long-press any entry, and then touch the **Delete** button.
  ➢ Swipe left on any of the entries, and then touch the Delete icon 🗑

Customize the journaling suggestions

Carry out any of the below:

❖ Adjust your privacy settings: Enter the Settings application, touch Privacy & Security, touch Journaling Suggestion, and then activate or deactivate any of the categories.
❖ Change the notifications settings: Enter the Settings application, touch Notifications, touch Journaling Suggestion, and then make the needed changes.
❖ Create new entries without having to see suggestions: Enter the Settings application, touch Journal, and then activate the **Skip Journaling Suggestion** feature.

Lock your journal

❖ Enter the Settings application, touch Journal, touch Lock Journal, and then adhere to the directives on your display.
❖ To unlock your journal, enter the Journal application, and then use Face ID or your iPhone's password

Create a journal plan

You can schedule journal notifications to help you form a habit.

❖ Enter the Settings application, touch Journal, touch Journal Schedule, and then activate Schedule.
❖ Select the days & time

Save videos & pictures captured in the Journal app

To save videos & pictures captured in the Journal application to the Photos application, enter the Settings application, touch Journal, and then activate the **Save to Photos** option.

Enable or disable Journal notifications

Enter the Settings app, touch Notification> Journal.

Save your journal entries to iCloud

❖ Enter the Settings application, touch [your name], and then touch iCloud.
❖ Touch the **Show All** button, and then activate Journal.

NOTES APP

In the Notes application, you can write down ideas or organize detailed information with check-lists, pictures, sketches, etc.

Create & format a new note

❖ Launch the Notes application, click on the Compose Notes icon 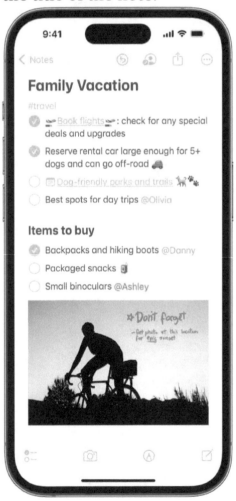, and then start typing in the text area.

The 1st line of the note will automatically become the title of the note.

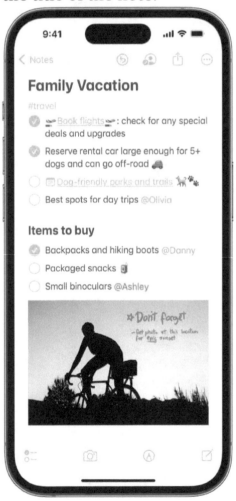

❖ Click on the Format button Aa to change the text format.
You can select one of the styles; use a numbered or bulleted list, & more.
❖ Click on the **Done** button to save the note on your device.

Touch the Checklist icon ⊘– in the note to add a checklist, after that type what you want, and tap the **Return** button to move to the next item.

Adding or editing a table

In the note, touch the Table button ⊞, and then carry out any of the below:

❖ Insert text: Tap one of the cells, and start typing. To enter text in another line in the same cell, just long-press the Shift button and tap on the **Next** button.
❖ Enter text in the next cell: Touch the **Next** button. When you get to the last cell, touch next to enter another row.
❖ Format, add, delete, or move a column or row: Touch the 3 dots at the beginning of the row or

above the column. Touch the 3 dots once more, and then choose any of the options.

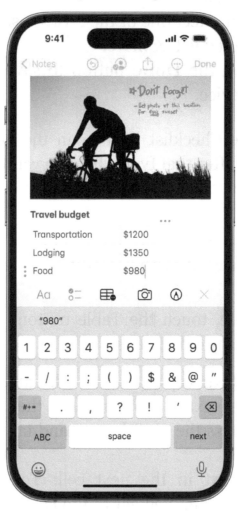

To delete a table and change the table's contents to text, tap one of the cells in the table, touch the Convert Table to Text button, and then touch the **Convert to Text** button.

Draw or write in a note

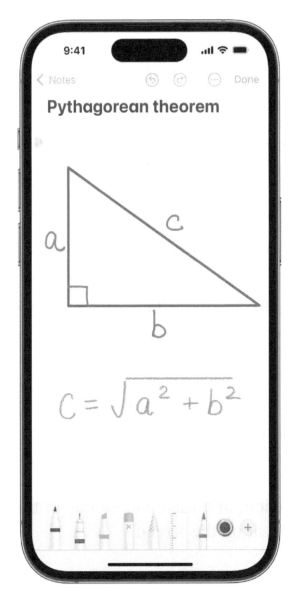

You can use your finger to draw or write in a note.

❖ Touch the Mark-up icon Ⓐ in a note, and then use a finger to write or draw.
❖ Carry out any of the below:
  ➢ You can change the handwriting area by dragging the resize handle (on the left) down or up.
  ➢ Change Markup tools or colours: Select the tool or colour you want from the Markup toolbar.

Select & edit handwriting & drawings

The Smart Selection feature allows iPhone users to select handwriting & drawings. You can delete, copy, or move the selection in the note.

❖ Touch the Lasso tool in the toolbar (the Lasso tool is between the ruler & eraser).
❖ Use the Lasso tool to draw a circle around an object to select the object.
❖ Touch the selection, and then choose one of the options that appear on the screen.

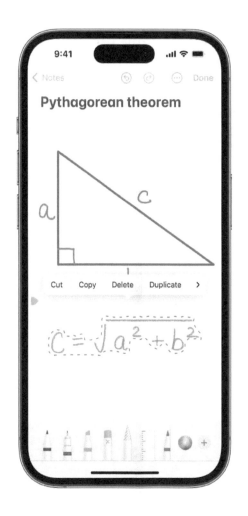

Scan text into a note using the camera

Use your iPhone camera to insert scanned text.

❖ Touch the Camera icon in a note, and then touch the **Scan Text** button.

❖ Set your phone in a way that the text in the document can be seen clearly from the camera screen.

❖ Select the text you want using the grab points, and then touch the **Insert** button.

Scan the document

❖ Touch the Camera icon  in a note, and then pick the **Scan Document** option.
❖ Set your phone in a way that the page of the document can be seen clearly from the camera screen—your device will automatically snap the page.

To manually snap the document, touch the White Shutter ○. Tap on the Flashlight icon ⚡ to switch the flashlight on or off.

❖ Scan more pages, and then touch the **Save** button when you are done.
The file will be stored in PDF format in the note.

Add a picture or video

❖ Click on the Camera button 📷 in a note.
❖ Select any of the videos or pictures from your Photos library, capture a new picture, or record a video.
To draw on a picture, touch the picture, touch the Markup icon Ⓐ, and then select from the available tools.
❖ To change an attachment's preview size, long-press the attachment, and then choose any of the options.

To store the videos & pictures captured in the Notes app in the Photos application, simply enter the Settings app, touch Notes, and then activate the **Save to Photos** feature.

Create Quick Notes anywhere on your phone

The Quick Notes feature allows you to easily write down thoughts over any application on your device.

All the Quick Notes you create are stored in the Notes application.

Create a Quick Note

Do any of the below to start a Quick Note from any application:

❖ Click on the Share button⬆, and then click on the **New Quick Note** button
❖ Swipe down from the upper right corner of the screen to enter the Controls Centre, then touch the Quick Notes icon🔲

(If you can't find the Quick Notes button🔲 in the Controls Centre, you can add it – simply enter the Settings app, touch Controls Centre, and then select Quick Notes.)

View all your Quick Notes

To see all the Quick Notes you've stored on your device, simply launch the Notes application, and touch Quick Notes in the folders list.

View all attachments in the Notes application

❖ At the top of the notes list, touch the More Options icon ⊙, and then touch the **View Attachment** button to show thumbnails of documents, pictures, etc.
❖ To open a note with a specific attachment, touch the thumbnail of the attachment, and then touch the **Show in Note** button.

Search for an item in a note

❖ Open the note
❖ Click on the More Options button ⊙, and then click on the **Find in Note** button
❖ Enter what you are looking for in the search box

Create, rename, move, or delete folders

Carry out any of the below in the folders list:

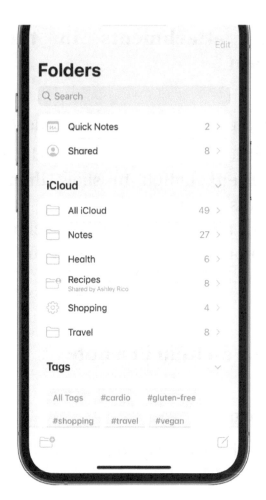

❖ Create a folder: Click on the New Folder button
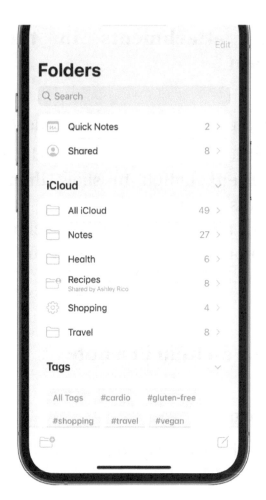, select any of your accounts (if you have multiple accounts), click on the **New Folder** button, and then give the folder a name.

❖ To create a subfolder, just long-press a folder, and then drag the folder onto another folder.

❖ To move a folder, just long-press the folder, and then drag the folder to another location on your display.
❖ Change the name of a folder: Long-press the folder, touch the **Rename** button, and then change the name of the folder.
❖ Delete a folder: Swipe the folder to the left, and then click on the Trash button 🗑 . Or long-press the folder, and then touch the **Delete** button

Move a note to another folder

Swipe the Note to the left, and then click on the Move button 🗁. Or, long-press the note, touch the **Move** button, and then select any of the folders.

Pin notes

You can pin a note to the top of the notes list, to do this, simply press & hold the note, and then click on the **Pin Note** button.

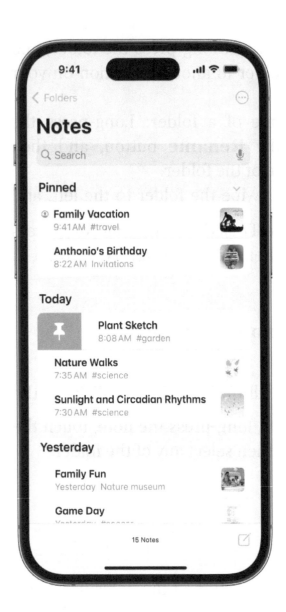

Delete a note

Swipe the Note to the left, and then click on the Trash button 🗑. Or long-press the note, and then touch the **Delete** button

Lock your notes

You can lock notes to protect your info.

Lock your notes with your iPhone's password or Face ID

❖ Enter the Settings application, touch Notes, and then touch Password.
❖ If you have more than one account, select the account you want to add a password to.
❖ Touch the **Use Device Passcode** button
❖ You can also activate Face ID.

Lock notes with a different password

You can create a unique password for locked notes to provide more security, but if you forget the password, you won't be able to gain access to locked notes.

- ❖ Enter the Settings application, touch Notes, and then touch Password.
- ❖ If you have more than one account, select the account you want to add a password to.
- ❖ Touch the **Custom Passcode** button
- ❖ You can also activate Face ID.

If you forget your custom password, you can reset it, but you will no longer be able to access your previously locked notes. The new password will apply to all locked notes henceforth. Enter the Settings application, touch Notes, touch Password, and then touch Reset Password.

Change the lock method

If you are making use of a unique password, you can switch to using your iPhone's password. Enter the Settings application, touch Notes, touch Passwords, select one of your accounts (if you have multiple accounts), and then touch the **Use Device Passcode** button.

Lock a note

You cannot lock notes that have videos, audio, PDF, Numbers, Pages, or Keynotes documents attached.

❖ Open a note, and then touch the More Options icon

❖ Touch the **Lock** button.

To remove a lock from a note, touch the More Options icon , and then touch the **Remove** button.

Open locked notes

Unlocking a locked note automatically unlocks all locked notes in the same account for a few minutes.

❖ Touch a locked note, and then touch the **View Note** button
❖ Use Face ID, or your iPhone's password to unlock the note.

Carry out any of the below to lock the note again:

❖ Touch the lock icon in the upper part of your display.
❖ Touch the **Lock Now** button in the lower part of the notes list.
❖ Exit the Notes application
❖ Lock your phone.

PASSCODE & FACE ID

Set a passcode

Set a passcode that has to be entered before your phone can be unlocked when you switch it on or wake it.

Set or change your passcode

- ❖ Enter the Settings app, and then touch the **Face ID and Passcode** button.
- ❖ Touch the **Turn On Pass code** button or the **Change Pass-code** button.
  Touch **Passcode Options** to see options for setting up a passcode.

Adjust when your phone automatically locks

Enter the Settings app, touch Display and Brightness, touch Auto Lock, and then choose one of the available options.

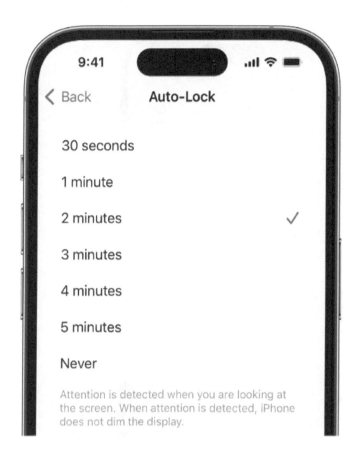

Erase your data after ten failed entries

Set your device to delete all info & personal settings after ten consecutive failed password entries.

❖ Enter the Settings app, and then touch the **Face ID and Passcode** button.
❖ Scroll down and then activate Erase Data.

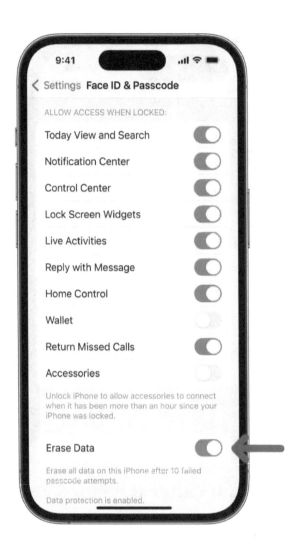

Disable the passcode

❖ Enter the Settings app, and then touch the **Face ID and Passcode** button.

❖ Touch **Turn Off Passcode**

Setup Face ID

With the **Face ID** feature, you can unlock your phone, authenticate purchases & payments, and log in to some 3rd-party applications by just staring at your iPhone's screen.

Setup Face ID or add another appearance

❖ If you did not configure the **Face ID** feature when setting up your phone, enter the Settings app, click on Face ID and Passcode, click Setup Face ID, and then adhere to the instructions on your display.
❖ To add another appearance, enter the Settings app, tap the **Face ID and Passcode** button, click Setup an Alternate Appearance, and then adhere to the instructions on your display.

Temporarily deactivate Face ID

You can temporarily stop Face ID from opening your phone.

❖ Press your iPhone's side button & a volume button simultaneously for about two seconds.

❖ When you see the sliders on the screen, press the side button to lock your device.

Face ID will be reactivated after you unlock your phone with your passcode.

Deactivate Face ID

❖ Enter the Settings app, and touch the **Face ID & Passcode** button.
❖ Carry out any of the below:
 ➢ Deactivate Face ID for certain things: Deactivate any of the options.
 ➢ Disable Face ID: Touch the **Reset Face ID** button.

Control access to info on your Lock screen

You can easily gain access to frequently used features (Controls Centre, Notifications Centre, etc.) from the lock screen even when your phone is locked.

If you deactivate Lock Screen access to a certain feature like Control Center, you and any other person who happens to use your iPhone will not be able to access the feature when your phone is locked.

Enter the Settings application, touch the **Face ID & Passcode** button, and then select the options in the **Allow Access When Locked** section.

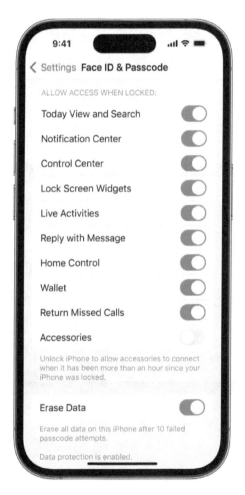

USE YOUR IPHONE WITH OTHER DEVICES

Use your phone as a webcam

You can use your phone as a microphone or webcam for your MacOS device, thereby taking advantage of your iPhone's powerful camera & video effects.

Note: Before you can make use of the **Continuity Camera** feature, you have to ensure your MacOS device & iPhone are using the same Apple ID. Additionally, you need to activate WiFi & Bluetooth on both devices.

Select an external camera on your Mac

❖ Use a cable to connect your iPhone or a camera to your Mac or connect it wirelessly.
❖ Launch an application that captures video, and then do any of the below:
  ➢ Photos booth: Click on the **Camera** button in the menus bar, then select your iPhone or any other available option.
  ➢ QuickTime Player: Click on File> New Movie Recording, hold your cursor over the window, click on the down arrow ⌄, and then choose your phone or any other available option as the camera.
  ➢ Face-Time: Click on the **Video** button in the menus bar, and then select your phone or any other available option.
  ➢ 3rd-party applications: You can use your iPhone with 3rd-party applications. To learn how, simply go through the developer's manual.

Use your phone as a microphone or webcam

❖ Place your iPhone on a stand or place the back camera on the same side as your Mac's screen. Your iPhone's screen shouldn't be visible to you & ensure your phone is in landscape orientation.

❖ Launch an application on your MacOS device that captures video or has access to the Mic.
❖ Follow the directives in the previous subheading to choose your iPhone as the microphone or camera in the application's settings or menu bar.
❖ You can carry out any of the below:
  ➢ Pause the audio or video: Click the **Pause** button on your phone. Or, unlock your phone.

- ➤ Resume the audio or video: Click on the **Resume** button on your iPhone. Or, lock your iPhone.
- ➤ Stop making use of your phone as a Mic or webcam: Exit & close the application on your Mac.
- ➤ Remove your phone as one of the options: Click on the **Disconnect** button on your phone, and then confirm that you'd like to disconnect.

To reconnect your phone, use a USB cable to connect it to your MacOS device.

Activate Video effects & Desk View

After using your phone as a webcam for your MacOS device, you can click on the Video icon in the menus bar and use any of the video conferencing features. For instance, Desk View displays a top-down view of your table, Studio Light makes the background dimmer & brightens your face, and Portrait Mode blurs the background and places the focus on you.

If you cannot find your phone as a Mic or camera option

If you cannot find your phone in the Mic or camera list in an application or Sound setting, try the following.

❖ Use a USB cable to connect your iPhone to your Mac & check one more time.
❖ Check the following:
  ➢ You have enabled Continuity Camera in the Setting app> General > AirPlay and Hand-off on your iPhone.
  ➢ Your phone sees the Mac as a trusted computer.
  ➢ You have enabled Bluetooth, WiFi, & 2-factor authentication on your MacOS device & iPhone
  ➢ Both devices are within Bluetooth range (30ft)
  ➢ Both devices are registered with the same Apple ID
  ➢ The video application you're using has been updated to the latest version.
  ➢ Your MacOS device is not sharing its internet connection and your phone is not sharing its mobile connection.

Handoff

The Handoff feature allows you to start something on one of your Apple devices (iPhone, iPad, etc.) & continue from where they stopped on another Apple device. For instance, you can start replying to an e-mail on your phone & complete it in the Mail app on your iMac. **Handoff** is compatible with many Apple applications, such as Safari, Contacts, & Calendar, and some 3rd-party applications.

Getting Started

Before you can use the Handoff feature, make sure of the below:

❖ Both devices are using the same Apple ID.
❖ You have activated Hand-off, Bluetooth, & WiFi on your Mac, iPhone, or any of your other Apple devices
❖ Both devices are within Bluetooth range (33ft)

Handoff from another Apple device to your iPhone

❖ Swipe up from the lower edge of the screen, and stop in the middle of the screen to show the Apps Switcher on your phone. You will find the Hand-off icon of the application you are using on your other Apple device in the lower part of the Apps Switcher on your iPhone.

❖ Touch the Hand-off icon to continue working in the application on your phone.

Handoff from your phone to another Apple device

On other Apple devices, touch or click on the Handoff icon to continue using the application.

You can find the Handoff icons for applications you are using on your phone in the following places on your other Apple devices:

❖ MacOS device: The right side of the Dock.

❖ iPad: on the Dock

Enable or disable Handoff on your Apple devices

❖ IPhone, iPod touch, & iPad: Enter the Settings app, tap General, tap AirPlay & Handoff, and then activate or disable Handoff.

❖ MacOS 13.0: Click on the Apple menu icon in the menu bar, click on System Settings in the menu that appears, click the **General** button in the sidebar, click on AirDrop & Handoff on the right of the window, and then enable or disable **Allow Handoff between this Mac & iCloud device**.

❖ MacOS 12.50 or before: Select Apple menu> Systems Preference, click the **General** button, and then select or unselect **Allow Hand-off between this Mac & iCloud device**.

Universal Clipboard

The Universal Clipboard feature allows Apple device users to copy or cut content from one Apple device & paste it onto another Apple device. For instance, you can copy a picture or text on your iPhone and paste it on your iMac, & vice versa.

Getting Started

Before you can use the Universal Clipboard feature, make sure of the below:

❖ Both devices are using the same Apple ID.
❖ You have activated Hand-off, Bluetooth, & WiFi on your MacOS device, iPhone, or any other Apple device
❖ Both devices are within Bluetooth range (33ft)

Copy, cut, or paste

❖ Cut: Pinch closed with 3 of your fingers twice.
❖ Copy: Pinch closed with 3 of your fingers
❖ Paste: Pinch open with 3 of your fingers

You can also long-press a block of highlighted text, and then touch **Copy**, **Cut**, or **Paste**.

TURN ON/OFF, RESTART, UPDATE, BACKUP, RESTORE & RESET

Switch on your phone

Long-press the Side button till you see the Apple icon on your display.

Switch off your phone

Do any of the below:

❖ Long-press the Side button & a Volume button till you see the sliders, then slide the Power-Off slider.

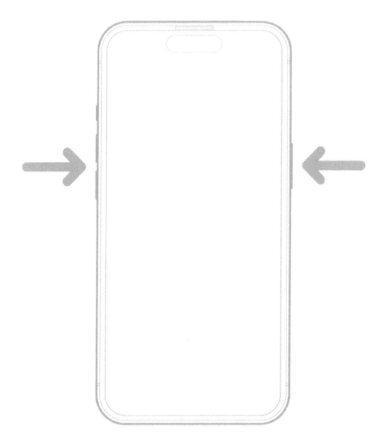

❖ Enter the Settings app, touch General, touch Shut Down, then slide the slider.

Force restart your phone

If your phone is unresponsive and you cannot switch it off, you can force it to restart.

- ❖ Press & release the Increase volume button.
- ❖ Press & release the Decrease volume button.
- ❖ Hold down the side button till you see the Apple symbol on your display.

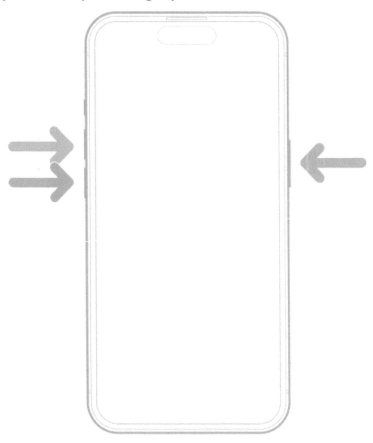

Update your iPhone's operating system

Before updating to the latest OS, ensure you backup your iPhone.

Update your phone automatically

❖ Navigate to the Settings app, click on General, touch Software Updates, and then click on Automatic Update.

❖ Enable iOS Update in the Automatically Install & Automatically Download sections

Update your phone manually

❖ Enter the Settings app, tap General, and then tap on Software Updates

Your screen will show the iOS version your iPhone is using at the moment and whether there's an update available.

Backup your iPhone

Backup your iPhone with your PC or iCloud.

Use iCloud to backup your phone

❖ Enter the Settings app, tap [your name], tap iCloud, and then tap iCloud Backup.
❖ Enable iCloud Backup.
ICloud will automatically backup your phone every day when it's locked, charging, and connected to WiFi.
Note: Your carrier may give you the option to backup your phone using mobile network. Enter the Settings app, tap [your name], tap iCloud,

tap iCloud Backup, and then activate or deactivate Backup Over Cellular.

❖ Touch the **Backup Now** button to back up your iPhone manually.

To see all your backups, launch the Settings app, tap [your name], tap iCloud, tap Manage Accounts Storage, and then tap Backups. To remove a backup, select one of the backups from the list and then touch the **Turn Off & Delete from iCloud** button.

Use your MacOS device to Backup your iPhone

❖ Use a USB cable to connect your phone to your MacOS device.

❖ Choose your iPhone in your Mac's Finder sidebar.

❖ Click on **General** in the upper part of the Finder window.

❖ Choose **Backup all iPhone data to this Mac.**

❖ Select "Encrypt local backup" to encrypt & password-protect the backup.

❖ Click on the **Backup Now** button.

Use your Windows PC to Backup your iPhone

❖ Use a USB cable to connect your phone to your PC.
❖ In the iTune application on your computer, click on the iPhone button in the upper left part of the iTunes window.
❖ Click on the **Summary** button.
❖ Click the **Backup Now** button in the Backups section.
❖ To encrypt the back up, choose "Encrypt backup", insert a passcode, and then click the **Set Password** button.

To view the backups saved on your PC, select Edit> Preference, and then click on **Device**.

Restore all content from a backup

Restore your phone from an iCloud backup

❖ Switch on your new or just erased phone.
❖ Touch the **Setup Manually** button, touch Restore from iCloud Back Up, and then adhere to the directives on your screen.

Restore your phone from a computer backup

❖ Use a USB cable to connect your new or just erased phone to the computer that has the backup.
❖ Carry out any of the below:
  ➢ On a Mac(macOS 10.150 or after): Choose your iPhone in the Mac's Finder sidebar, click the **Trust** button, and then click the **Restore from this Back up** button.
  ➢ On a Windows computer or a Mac (macOS 10.140 or before): Launch the iTunes application, click on the iPhone icon in the upper left part of the iTunes window, click the **Summary** button, and then click the **Restore Back up** button.
❖ Select one of the backups from the list, and then click the **Continue** button.

If the backup is password-protected, you must type your password before you can restore your settings & files.

Reset iPhone settings to defaults

You can return your iPhone's settings to their defaults without deleting your content.

❖ Enter the Settings app, touch General, tap Transfer or Reset iPhone, and then tap Reset.
❖ Select any of the options:
  ➢ Reset the keyboard dictionary.
  ➢ Reset all settings
  ➢ Reset location and privacy
  ➢ Reset the Home Screen Layout.
  ➢ Reset Network Settings

Erase iPhone

Erase your phone to permanently delete your content & settings.

❖ Launch the Settings app, tap General, and then tap Transfer or Reset iPhone
❖ Carry out any of the below:
  ➢ Prepare to move your contents to your new iPhone: Touch the **Get Started** button, and then adhere to the instructions on the screen. Once you're done, launch the Settings app, tap General, tap Transfer or Reset iPhone,

and then touch the **Erase All Contents & Settings** button.

➢ Erase all data from your phone: Touch the **Erase All Contents & Settings** button.

INDEX

Page | 519

276, 287, 290, 295,
389, 390, 495, 510

W

wallpaper, 102, 203, 204
Wallpaper, 101, 102, 202,
203, 204, 206
webcam, 498, 500, 501
widget, 118, 119, 120, 122,
123

WiFi, 15, 44, 45, 81, 82,
126, 168, 180, 223, 227,
241, 337, 339, 438, 499,
502, 503, 507, 512

Z

zoom, 10, 26, 153, 162,
163, 203, 266, 281, 290,
294, 308, 309, 318,
437, 440, 441, 448, 449

Made in United States
Troutdale, OR
05/02/2024

19587718R00309